D0210369

אב AV

תשעה באב 9
Tisha Be-Av

תמוז TAMMUZ

סיון SIVAN

שבועות 6
Shavuot

אייר IYAR

יום העצמאות
Yom
Ha-Atsma-ut 5

ניסן NISAN

יום השואה 27
Yom
Ha-Sho-ah

פסח 15
Pesach

בתולה
VIRGO
LEO
Summer קיץ
CANCER
GEMINI
Spring אביב
TAURUS
ARIES

n leapyears)

Gates
of the Seasons

אֵלֶּה מוֹעֲדֵי יְיָ מִקְרָאֵי קֹדֶשׁ
אֲשֶׁר־תִּקְרְאוּ אֹתָם בְּמוֹעֲדָם.

These are the set times of the Lord,
the sacred occasions which you shall celebrate
each at its appointed time.

—LEVITICUS 23:4

שַׁעֲרֵי מוֹעֵד
Gates of the Seasons

A GUIDE TO THE
JEWISH YEAR

Edited by
Peter S. Knobel

With notes by
Bennett M. Hermann
and
Peter S. Knobel

Illustrated by Ismar David

CENTRAL CONFERENCE OF AMERICAN RABBIS

5743   NEW YORK   1983

LIBRARY OF CONGRESS CATALOGING IN PUBLICATION DATA
Main entry under title:

Gates of the Seasons

In English. Includes benedictions in English and Hebrew with Romanization. Includes bibliography and references.

1. Reform Judaism—Customs and practices. 2. Fasts and feasts—Judaism. I. Knobel, Peter S., 1943–
II. Hermann, Bennett M. III. Central Conference of American Rabbis. IV. Title: *Sha'are Mo'ed*.

BM 700.G35   1983   296.4'3   83-7527

ISBN 0-916694-92-5 (pbk.)

This book was produced by the Committee on Reform Jewish
Practice of the Central Conference of American Rabbis
W. Gunther Plaut, Chairman, 1972–1981
Simeon J. Maslin, Chairman, 1981–

Norman J. Cohen   Michael A. Signer
Joan S. Friedman   Michael S. Stroh
Peter S. Knobel   Brooks R. Susman
Seymour Prystowsky   Eric H. Yoffie
Aaron Rosenberg

Ex Officio:

Herbert Bronstein   Walter Jacob
Lawrence A. Hoffman

Copy editing and book design provided by:
SPECIAL EDITION, P.O. Box 09553,
Columbus, Ohio 43209 (614/231-4088)

CONTENTS

FOREWORD

WHAT? Another book on Jewish practices from the Reform Movement? *A Shabbat Manual* in 1972; then the new prayerbook with its constant refrain "Be mindful of all my *mitzvot* . . . " in 1975; *Gates of the House* with a whole variety of home rituals and services in 1977; and, of course, *Gates of Mitzvah* (A Guide to the Jewish Life Cycle) in 1979. What is happening to the Reform Movement?!

There has been an undeniable trend toward the reinstitution of traditional practices in Reform Judaism during the past decade. And so, one has every right to ask where the Reform Movement is going. Is it, as many claim, returning to Orthodoxy? And is this latest publication, with its many suggestions for the celebration of Sabbaths and festivals, symptomatic of that return?

In order to answer these questions properly, one must begin with an understanding of what Reform Judaism really is. It would be simplistic to define our movement on the basis of more or less ritual observances. It is our philosophy of Judaism that makes us Reform Jews. Particular ritual practices which, on the one hand, do not negate our philosophy and which, on the other, reinforce and enrich our Judaism are not only acceptable in Reform, they are desirable.

As Reform Jews, we are free to take upon ourselves the performance of certain customs and ceremonies and to reject others. We do not believe that revelation happened at one moment in ancient history and that we are bound today by the way that a pre-scientific civilization understood that revelation. A beautiful passage in the old *Union Prayerbook* teaches us that we should

> welcome all truth, whether shining from the annals of ancient revelation or reaching us through the seers of our own time, for Thou hidest not Thy light from any generation of Thy children that yearn for Thee and seek Thy guidance.

In this book, as in *Gates of Mitzvah*, certain ancient practices are recommended and others are not. Equally important, though, is the fact that certain *new* practices are also recommended as *mitzvot*—the bringing of female babies into the *Berit* and the observances of Yom HaSho-ah and Yom Ha-Atsma-ut come readily to mind. Those customs of long-standing which still have meaning and which add beauty and Jewish depth to our lives should be observed. But, as Reform Jews, we have every right to discard practices which have lost meaning for contemporary Jews and which lack an aesthetic dimension. It is our duty to study each and every tradition and, on the basis of that study, either to adopt it or to reject it. And it is our duty also to find new and contemporary modes for the expression of inchoate spiritual feelings.

We must never forget, though, that we are first and foremost Jews, related to four thousand years of Jewish history and related to thirteen million Jews the world over. Therefore, *the burden of proof must always be on those who want to abandon a particular tradition, not on those who want to retain it.* Without strong links to the vast body of Jewish tradition, we may be good people but we are certainly not good Jews capable of transmitting Judaism to the next generation.

This volume, *Gates of the Seasons*, is the creation of the CCAR's Committee on Reform Jewish Practice and, more particularly, of its editor, Rabbi Peter Knobel. Rabbi Knobel devoted countless hours over a three-year period to this volume and was always receptive to suggestions by members of the committee and by colleagues in the CCAR. We owe him a debt of gratitude as we do also to Rabbi W. Gunther Plaut, who guided the committee in its first years and originally conceived this sacred project. Thanks are due also to Rabbi Bennett Hermann, who did much of the original research on the notes to this volume, and to Rabbi Elliot Stevens, whose expert advice guided the committee from the day this book was conceived through its publication.

While *Gates of Mitzvah* covers the Jewish life cycle, this new volume—*Gates of the Seasons*—deals with the Jewish calendar. With these two volumes, however, we have by no means exhausted the possibilities for *mitzvot* within our Jewish tradition. We have not even touched upon the vast field of ethical *mitzvot*—business ethics, family ethics, medical ethics, etc. We look forward to the publication someday soon of a volume on ethics from a Reform Jewish point of view. Our purpose in these two volumes was not to include every possible *mitzvah*, but rather to describe and recommend those *mitzvot* of the Jewish life cycle and the Jewish calendar that might add depth and beauty to the lives of modern Jews.

It is our *mitzvot*—our traditional and particular Jewish practices— that put us in touch with Abraham, Moses, Esther, and the Jews of fifth-century Babylonia, twelfth-century Spain, eighteenth-century Poland, and twentieth-century Auschwitz. It is the study and the practice of our *mitzvot* that has "kept us in life, sustained us, and brought us to this moment."

SIMEON J. MASLIN, CHAIRMAN
Committee on Reform Jewish Practice

Elul, 5743
August, 1983

RELIGIOUS PRACTICE

JUDAISM emphasizes action rather than creed as the primary expression of a religious life, the means by which we strive to achieve universal justice and peace. Reform Judaism shares this emphasis on duty and obligation. Our founders stressed that the Jew's ethical responsibilities, personal and social, are enjoined by God. The past century has taught us that the claims made upon us may begin with our ethical obligations, but they extend to many other aspects of Jewish living, including creating a Jewish home centered on family devotion, lifelong study, private prayer and public worship, daily religious observance, keeping the Sabbath and the holy days, celebrating the major events of life, involvement with the synagogue and community, and other activities which promote the survival of the Jewish people and enhance its existence. Within each area of Jewish observance, Reform Jews are called upon to confront the claims of Jewish tradition, however differently perceived, and to exercise their individual autonomy, choosing and creating on the basis of commitment and knowledge.

—From the "Centenary Perspective,"
adopted by the Central Conference
of American Rabbis in 1976.

Introduction

These are My festivals, the festivals
of the Lord, which you shall proclaim
as sacred occasions.

—LEVITICUS 23:2

THE CYCLE OF THE JEWISH YEAR

AS the earth rotates upon its axis, night becomes day and day turns once again into night. As the earth revolves around the sun, autumn gives way to winter, winter yields to spring, spring blossoms into summer, summer once again becomes fall. The moon also exhibits cyclical changes, waxing and waning at regular intervals. The rhythmic movements of the celestial bodies divide the endless flow of time into days, months, and years. By monitoring these repetitions, we have established a calendar to measure the passage of time. The calendar rules our lives, telling us when to work and when to rest, differentiating special days from ordinary days.*

As Jews living in the Diaspora, two calendars regulate our lives, the civil and the Jewish. For us the days, the months, and the years bear two dates and two distinct rhythms. This volume, *Gates of the Seasons—A Guide to the Jewish Year*, is designed to help Jews feel more clearly the flow of Jewish time.

Every day of the week points toward Shabbat[1]—day of rest, day of joy, day of holiness. Each year begins in the fall with Rosh Hashanah. The blast of the *Shofar* ushers in the New Year, announcing the season of repentance. Yom Kippur follows with its day-long fast and majestic liturgy. We confess our sins and become reconciled with God so that we can begin the new year free from accumulated guilt. Then Sukkot, the joyous celebration of the harvest, reminder of the ancient journey of our people to the Land of Israel, arrives rich with agricultural symbolism.

However, soon fall becomes winter, and the dark nights are illuminated by the brightly burning lights of Chanukah, recalling for us the heroic Maccabees and our people's long struggle to remain Jewish. As winter nears its end, we read the Purim story from the *Megilah*, and we revel in the miracle of our physical survival despite the numerous attempts to destroy us.

Spring liberates the world from the grip of winter, and we recall our liberation from Egyptian bondage. We gather at the Pesach table

*See the essay "The Jewish Calendar" which follows this section.

to recite the *Hagadah*, to eat the symbolic foods, and to renew our commitment to the liberation of all humanity. From Passover we count seven weeks to Shavuot. During this period, on Yom HaShoah, we mourn the death of six million Jews slaughtered by the Nazis, but our grief gives way to rejoicing when we join in the celebration of Israel's rebirth on Yom Ha-Atsma-ut. The counting ends with Shavuot, the festival which celebrates revelation. We stand as at Mt. Sinai with our ancestors, again receiving Torah and entering into the covenant with God.

Summer is soon upon us, and on Tish-ah Be-Av we recall the tragic destructions of the Temples and two periods of sovereignty over the Land of Israel and lament the historic suffering of our people. Then—the dark mood turns to anticipation as we enter the month of Elul and prepare again to greet the New Year, with Rosh Hashanah.

Gates of the Seasons, like *Gates of Mitzvah*, proceeds from the premise that *mitzvah* is the key to authentic Jewish existence and to the sanctification of life. This book, too, was conceived to help Jews make Jewish responses and to give their lives Jewish depth and character. As Reform Jews, our philosophy is based on the twin commitments to Jewish continuity and to personal freedom of choice.

The edifice of Jewish living is constructed of *mitzvot*. As a building is constructed one brick at a time, so is a significant Jewish life. Our Sages recognized that the observance of one *mitzvah* leads to the observance of others. As Ben Azzai said: "One *mitzvah* brings another in its wake."[2] The secret of observing *mitzvot* is to begin.

THE JEWISH CALENDAR

ALEXANDER GUTTMANN

IN order to appreciate fully the meaning of the Jewish holidays—their relationships to the seasons, to historical events, and to each other—it is necessary to have a basic understanding of the Jewish calendar. One often hears people remark: "The holidays are early this year," or: "Reform Jews don't celebrate the second day." From where did the Jewish calendar come? How does it work? What is its significance for us?

The main purpose of the Jewish calendar is, and always has been, to set the dates of the festivals. Our present calendar has its roots in the Torah, but it has been modified by Jewish religious authorities through the ages. The principal rules were established by the Sages and Rabbis of antiquity and were supplemented by medieval scholars. In Talmudic times the regulation of the calendar was the exclusive right of the Jewish leadership in the Land of Israel, particularly that of the *Nasi* (Patriarch).[3] Since that time, such regulation has been regarded as a task of crucial importance for the observance of Judaism.

The Structure of the Jewish Calendar

The point of departure in regulating the Jewish calendar is the Biblical law, "Observe the month of *Aviv* and keep the Passover to the Lord your God" (Deuteronomy 16:1). Passover, therefore, must fall every year in the spring at the time of *Aviv* (specifically, the appearance of the ripening ears of barley). And so, each year the ancient Jewish authorities watched for signs of the approaching spring. If these signs were late, they added an extra month of thirty days (called Adar II) to the year, before the Passover month.[4] Once the time of Passover had been established, the dates of all subsequent festivals would be determined based upon whether or not an extra month (a second Adar) had been added.

In the Bible, the Hebrew months are lunar (i.e., each month begins with the "birth" of the new moon). However, since festivals such as Passover and Sukkot had to occur in the proper agricultural season (i.e., according to the solar year), it is obvious that the Jewish calendar must be lunar solar. This means that the lunar year (approximately 354 days) and the solar year (approximately 365 days) had to be harmonized and adjusted to each other, a complex process that was meticulously refined by the ancient and medieval Rabbis.

The Jewish day has twenty-four hours and starts in the evening.[5] The length of the lunar month is traditionally calculated as 29 days, 12 hours, and 793 parts of an hour (divided into 1080 parts). This is the time span between one new moon and the next. Since it is impractical to start a new month at varying hours of the day, the Sages of antiquity ordained that the length of the month should alternate between 29 and 30 days. Since the lunar month is somewhat longer than 29 days and 12 hours, the remainder is taken care of by making the months of Cheshvan and Kislev flexible, i.e., they can both have either 29 or 30 days.

The introduction of a permanent Jewish calendar became increasingly urgent after Jews began to spread throughout the world. As Jewry dispersed, regular contacts with the Jewish leadership in the Land of Israel, which had the sole privilege of regulating the calendar, became more and more difficult. The most important step in this process of permanent calendar reform was the adoption in the eighth century C.E. of a nineteen-year cycle of "intercalation" (i.e., harmonization of the solar and lunar calendars). The adoption of this cycle made the actual physical observation of the new moon and the signs of approaching spring unnecessary. This cycle of nineteen years adjusts the lunar year to the solar year by inserting into it seven leap years (i.e., the additional 30-day month of Adar) in the following order: every third, sixth, eighth, eleventh, fourteenth, seventeenth, and nineteenth year.[6]

In the Bible the months are most frequently designated by ordinal numbers. However, there are references both to such ancient names as Ziv, Eitanim, and Aviv and to some of the now customary names Kislev, Tevet, Adar, Nisan, Sivan, and Elul, which are of Babylonian origin.[7] But, it is only since the first century that the Hebrew calendar has employed the now traditional month names of Nisan, Iyar, Sivan, Tamuz, Av, Elul, Tishri, Cheshvan, Kislev, Tevet, Shevat, and Adar.

A.D., A.M., B.C., and B.C.E.

The Jewish tradition of counting years since the creation of the world has its roots in early Talmudic times, but it was not adopted authoritatively until several centuries later. In Biblical times, dates were referred to as being "two years before the earthquake," "the year of the death of King Uzziah," etc. In Talmudic times we find instances of dating from the creation of the world,[8] but this was adopted as *the* Jewish method only much later as a response to Christian dating.

It was in the eighth century that Christians began to date their documents generally as A.D. (*Anno Domini*, the year of the Lord), and so it is hardly a coincidence that in the eighth and ninth centuries we find more and more Jewish documents dated "since the creation of the world" (sometimes referred to as A.M., *Anno Mundi*, the year of the world). Obviously, calculating dates based on the Christian theological principles was not acceptable to Jews; nevertheless, it was not until the twelfth century that dating "since the creation" was accepted by Jews universally.

Only a minority of Jews today would take the traditional Jewish date as being literally "since the creation of the world." Most of us accept the findings of science which indicate that our world is billions of years old, rather than some 5700. But the date that changes each year with Rosh Hashanah is a convenient reference point to the beginnings of Jewish history and relates us to a venerable tradition.

Jewish texts will often use such designations as B.C.E. (Before the Common, or Christian, Era) or C.E. in order to avoid any dating related to Christianity. In order to determine the Jewish year for a given civil year, the number 3760 is added; conversely, in order to find the civil year for a given Jewish year, 3760 is subtracted. Of course, since the Jewish year changes with Rosh Hashanah, the number to work with from Rosh Hashanah to December 31 is 3761.

The Second Days of the Festivals

The greatest change which the Rabbis made in the festival calendar was the addition of a day to each of the holidays ordained in the Torah, except Yom Kippur. This was done in the early Talmudic period (i.e., first century). Compelling circumstances at that time forced the Rabbis to make this change.

Not only was the confirmation and sanctification of the new moon—and therefore the new month—the duty of the Palestinian authorities, but theirs was also the task of communicating the dates of the new moons to every Jewish community. This was a task of vital importance, as the new moon determines the dates of the festivals. At an earlier time, the new moon (i.e., the first of the month) was communicated to all the Jews in Palestine and the Diaspora by kindling flares on hilltops. However, after the Samaritans kindled flares at the wrong time to confuse the Jews, the news about the New Moon had to be communicated by messengers.[9] The change was introduced by Judah Hanasi (c. 135–200 C.E.).[10]

Since it often happened that the messengers did not arrive in time at the places of their destination outside of Palestine because of road hazards, wars, or political upheavals, a second day was added to the holidays for the Jews in the Diaspora. This assured that one of the two days on which they celebrated the festival was indeed the proper holy day. In Palestine the addition of these "second days" to the festivals was not necessary because the news about the sighting of the new moon, proclaimed in Palestine,[11] reached every part of that land in due time, i.e., prior to the dates of the festivals. The exception was Rosh Hashanah, which falls on the first day of the month of Tishri, making timely communication about this New Moon, even in Palestine, impossible.[12]

During the Talmudic period a stable, scientifically determined calendar was adopted, and so the pragmatic need for "second days" disappeared. But the Palestinian authorities did not abolish these extra days of observance for Diaspora Jews (nor the second day of Rosh Hashanah for Palestinian Jews) because of the Rabbinic principle that we "may not change the custom of [our] forefathers."[13]

Reform Judaism, from its very inception, abolished the "second days" of the festivals[14] and returned to the observance of seven one-day festivals as ordained in the Torah—i.e., the first day of Passover (Leviticus 23:7, and elsewhere), the seventh day of Passover (Lev. 23:8), Shavuot (Lev. 23:21), Rosh Hashanah (Lev. 23:24), Yom

Kippur (Lev. 23:27), the first day of Sukkot (Lev. 23:35), and Shemini Atseret (Lev. 23:36). However, except for the "second days," Reform Judaism has always celebrated the festivals according to the traditional calendar. In effect, this means that Reform Jews today celebrate the festivals according to the religious calendar observed in Israel, with the one exception of the second day of Rosh Hashanah (which is observed by a minority of Reform congregations).

In Jewish life the practice of *mitzvot*, particularly those *mitzvot* which are the essence of this book, has always been as important as theology. This is true not only in our time but was so in former times as well. Quite illuminating in this respect is a surprising bit of dialogue from the Middle Ages: Jacob Al-Kirkisani (10th century C.E.), a famous Karaite, asked Jacob ben Ephraim of Palestine, "You [Rabbanites] draw near the Isunians and intermarry with them, though you yourself know that they ascribe prophecy to men who did not possess it, to Jesus, Mohammed, and Abu Isa." Jacob ben Ephraim replied, "[We do so] because they do not differ with us with regard to the *festivals*."[15]

One can learn more about the observance of Judaism through a study of the holy days and their customs than through any other particular aspect of Judaism. Indeed, both the traditional and the liberal Jew would agree that "the catechism of the Jew is his calendar."[16]

EVERY DAY

JUDAISM provides rich opportunities to transform the ordinary into the sacred. The *mitzvot* of Shabbat and the festivals sanctify certain days by linking them to significant moments in Jewish history or to important Judaic concepts. The same may be said of the *mitzvot* which mark the various stages of the Jewish life cycle. While this volume concentrates on the *mitzvot* of Shabbat and the festivals, the practice of Judaism is not limited to special occasions. Judaism is lived every day.

According to Jewish tradition, *mitzvot* may be divided into two general categories: those which define the divine-human relationship (*Mitzvot bein adam lamakom*) and those which define the proper relationship between individuals and society (*Mitzvot bein adam lachavero*). While space does not permit an adequate treatment of either of these categories, a few examples will suffice to indicate the comprehensive nature of *mitzvah*.

Daily prayer,[17] table blessings,[18] and Torah study[19] are an integral part of Jewish living and would be classified as belonging to the category of *mitzvot* which deal with the divine-human relationship. Honoring one's parents,[20] honesty in business transactions,[21] loving one's neighbor,[22] and judging impartially[23] are but a few of the *mitzvot* which define a person's obligations to society. The two categories are not separate; they complement and amplify each other. For example, Torah study teaches us to behave ethically and at the same time teaches us to observe the festivals. The prophets denounce a society in which ritual takes precedence over ethics.[24] The task of joining ritual and ethics is the task of the Jew every day. Therefore, a volume on the *mitzvot* of Shabbat and the festivals must begin with the concept of the sanctification of every day.

Rabbi Eliezer taught, "Repent one day before your death." But his disciples asked, "How is it possible to repent one day before death, since no one knows on what day one will die?" Therefore, taught Rabbi Eliezer, live each day as though it were your last.[25]

שַׁבָּת

Shabbat

The people of Israel shall keep Shabbat,
observing Shabbat throughout the generations as
a covenant for all time. It shall be a sign for all
times between Me and the people of Israel. For
in six days God made heaven and earth and on
the seventh day God ceased from work and was
refreshed.

—EXODUS 31:16–17

Remember the Shabbat and keep it holy. . . . For
in six days the Lord made heaven and earth and
sea, and all that is in them, and God rested on
the seventh day; therefore the Lord blessed
Shabbat day and hallowed it.

—EXODUS 20:8–11

Observe Shabbat and keep it holy. . . .
Remember that you were a slave in the land of
Egypt and the Lord your God freed you from
there with a mighty hand and an outstretched
arm; therefore the Lord your God has
commanded you to observe the Shabbat day.

—DEUTERONOMY 5:12–15

SHABBAT is a unique Jewish contribution to our civilization. It is a weekly respite from endless toil and competition. Interrupting the pursuit of wealth and power, it turns the Jew toward the meaning of human existence. Given a day without labor, the individual can concentrate on being a creature fashioned in the divine image. On Shabbat we take delight in the beauty of creation, spending time with family, friends, and community and recharging our physical and spiritual batteries for the week ahead.

The recovery of Shabbat observance is a primary goal of this book. Jewish authenticity and a life of *mitzvah* are inexorably bound up with Shabbat observance. By celebrating Shabbat as an island of holy time in a sea of secular activity, the Jewish people have been able to survive the forces of assimilation and corruption. So crucial is Shabbat to Jewish survival that Achad Ha-am was moved to say, "More than Israel has kept Shabbat, Shabbat has kept Israel."[26]

The essential themes of Jewish theology—Creation, Revelation, and Redemption—are woven into the fabric of Shabbat liturgy and practice. Words and deeds, performing certain acts and refraining from others make Shabbat unique, significant, and joyous. Volumes have been written to extol and explain Shabbat (see "For Further Reading," pages 199–200). What follows are a few brief and simple observations.

The two different versions of the Ten Commandments in Exodus and Deuteronomy provide different reasons for the observance of Shabbat. In Exodus it is connected with Creation,[27] and in Deuteronomy with the Exodus from Egypt.[28] Shabbat is a day on which we celebrate both the emergence of the world from chaos to order and the emergence of the Jewish people from slavery to freedom.

Shabbat is God's time, the God who created the world and who created Israel. Every Shabbat, when we lift the *Kiddush* cup for blessing, we remember the One who created the universe[29] and blessed our people with freedom.[30]

As a reminder of Creation, Shabbat affords us a singular opportunity to reflect on the marvel of the universe and to contemplate our part in the continuing process of life. As sojourners, and not owners of the world, ours is the role of caretakers and preservers, not exploiters and destroyers. As a reminder of the Exodus from Egypt, Shabbat commits us to the ideals of freedom and justice. Having experienced bondage and degradation as well as liberation, we become attuned to the needs of others. Thus, Shabbat becomes a model of the way the world *could* be, the way that we can help to transform it as God's partners.

Our understanding of Shabbat can be further enhanced by recognizing another difference between the two versions of the Ten Commandments. Exodus 20:8 begins with the word *Zachor*, "Remember," implying cognition; Deuteronomy 5:12 opens with the word *Shamor*, "Observe," implying action. *Zachor* requires a spiritual, and *Shamor* a physical response. The former prescribes rest as an act of sanctification, and the latter prescribes it as an avoidance of labor.

An understanding of the deeper meaning of work and rest in today's society is essential to any real observance and enjoyment of Shabbat (see "Shabbat as Protest," pages 145–146, and A–5 below). A primary goal of Shabbat observance is the avoidance of gainful work and of all such activities which do not contribute to the celebration of Shabbat as a day of joy (*Oneg*), a day of holiness (*Kedushah*), and a day of rest (*Menuchah*). Shabbat is a day of leisure in which time is used to express our humanness. Through prayer and song, study and reflection, we celebrate the sanctity of Shabbat. The rest and joy of Shabbat provide opportunities for thoughtful re-evaluation and new perspective, for defining and recognizing goals. Once a week we are called upon to cease the struggle of extracting a living from the world and are summoned to pay attention to the inner core of our existence.

Our focus on Shabbat is on persons, not things. The cacophony of the daily struggle should give way to the symphony of life. On Shabbat we acquire an extra soul[31] which enables us to appreciate more fully our families, friends, and ourselves. We experience the pleasure of being a part of the community of Israel reaching toward perfection. Shabbat is a day which points toward the future. It is a day of hope and anticipation of the Messianic fulfillment which the Talmud describes as *"Yom shekulo Shabbat,"* a time of eternal Shabbat.[32]

SHABBAT*

A-1   The *mitzvah* of Shabbat observance

It is a *mitzvah* for every Jew, single or married, young or old, to observe Shabbat. The unique status of Shabbat is demonstrated by its being the only one of the holy days to be mentioned in the Ten Commandments.[33] Its observance distinguishes the Jewish people as a Covenant People.

> The people of Israel shall keep Shabbat, observing Shabbat throughout their generations as a covenant for all time. It is a sign for all time between Me and the people of Israel.
> (Exodus 31:16–17)

מִצְוֹת Shabbat observance involves both positive and negative *mitzvot*, i.e., doing and refraining from doing.

A-2   The *mitzvah* of joy (*Oneg*)

עֹנֶג It is a *mitzvah* to take delight in Shabbat observance, as Isaiah said, "You shall call Shabbat a delight" (58:13). *Oneg* implies celebration and relaxation, sharing time with loved ones, enjoying the beauty of nature, eating a leisurely meal made special with conviviality and song, visiting with friends and relatives, taking a leisurely stroll, reading, and listening to music. All of these are appropriate expressions of *Oneg*. Because of the special emphasis on *Oneg*, Jewish tradition recommended sexual relations between husband and wife on Shabbat.[34]

A simple list of activities is not adequate to describe *Oneg*; it is a total atmosphere which is created by those activities which refresh the body and the spirit and promote serenity.

---

*The following list of *mitzvot* is a revision of the earlier "Catalogue of Shabbat Opportunities," *A Shabbat Manual* (New York: Central Conference of American Rabbis, 1972), pages 9–13.

A-3   The *mitzvah* of sanctification (*Kedushah*)

It is a *mitzvah* to hallow Shabbat by setting it apart from the other days of the week. The Torah depicts Shabbat as the culmination of Creation and describes God as blessing

שַׁבָּת קֹדֶשׁ   it and sanctifying it (making it *Shabbat Kodesh*).[35] Every Jew should partake of this day's special nature and abstain from that which lessens his or her awareness of its distinctive character. Shabbat must be distinguished from the other days of the week so that those who observe it may

קְדוּשָׁה   be transformed by its holiness (*Kedushah*).

A-4   The *mitzvah* of rest (*Menuchah*)

It is a *mitzvah* to rest on Shabbat. However, Shabbat rest

מְנוּחָה   (*Menuchah*) implies much more than simply refraining from work (see A-5 below).[36] The concept of Shabbat rest includes both physical relaxation (for example, a Shabbat afternoon nap) and tranquility of mind and spirit. On Shabbat one deliberately turns away from weekday pressures and activities. The pace of life on Shabbat should be different from the rest of the week.

Conversations should not focus on the problems of everyday existence but rather on the meaning of life and the awareness of beauty in God's creation.[37] One might choose, for example, to walk more slowly on Shabbat in order to absorb one's surroundings and to enjoy the relaxed atmosphere of Shabbat.[38]

If the week is characterized by competition, rush, and turmoil, their absence will contribute to serenity and to the rejuvenation of body and spirit. It is this unique quality of *Menuchah* which moves our tradition to call Shabbat "a foretaste of the days of the Messiah."[39]

A-5   The *mitzvah* of refraining from work

It is a *mitzvah* to refrain from work on Shabbat, as it is said: "Six days you shall labor and do all your work, but the seventh day is a Shabbat to the Lord your God; on it you shall not do any work" (Exodus 20:8–10). Abstinence from work is a major expression of Shabbat observance;* however, it is no simple matter to define work today.[40] Certain activities which some do to earn a living, others do for relaxation or to express their creativity. Clearly, though, one should avoid one's normal occupation or profession on Shabbat whenever possible and engage only in those types of activities which enhance the *Oneg* (joy), *Menuchah* (rest), and *Kedushah* (holiness) of the day (see the essay "Shabbat as Protest," pages 145–146).

A-6 Social events during Shabbat worship hours

It is inappropriate to schedule social events at a time which conflicts with the Shabbat worship hours set by the congregation, and thereby to cause friends and relatives to choose between joining the congregation in worship or attending the event. One should not attend social events scheduled for these hours. Jewish organizations should be particularly careful in this matter.

A-7 Public events on Shabbat

The scheduling of, or participation in, public events on Shabbat violates the sanctity of Shabbat. Therefore, it may become necessary to object to civic functions on Shabbat, especially those which conflict with Shabbat worship hours, and to refuse participation in them. Observance of Shabbat is an obligation for young people as well as adults. Children should not attend public functions which conflict with Shabbat worship hours, whether sponsored by the school or other public bodies.

*Where circumstances require an individual to perform work on the Shabbat, that individual should nevertheless bear in mind that refraining from work is a major goal of Shabbat observance and he/she should perform as many Shabbat *mitzvot* as possible.

A-8 The *mitzvah* of avoiding activities which violate or appear to violate the sanctity of Shabbat

> It is a *mitzvah* to avoid all public activity which violates or gives the appearance of violating the sanctity of Shabbat.[41] Care should be taken to avoid conduct or participation in public activities which will offend other Jews. The guiding principle of Shabbat activities should be the enhancing of the distinctive Shabbat qualities of *Kedushah, Menuchah,* and *Oneg.*

A-9 The *mitzvah* of preparation

> It is a *mitzvah* to prepare for Shabbat. According to the Rabbis, this *mitzvah* is implied in the Exodus version of the Ten Commandments, "Remember Shabbat and keep it holy" (Exodus 20:8).[42] Preparations may begin well before Shabbat by buying special foods[43] or waiting to wear a new garment for Shabbat.[44]
>
> Jewish tradition compares the arrival of Shabbat to the arrival of an important guest.[45] Therefore, before the beginning of Shabbat special preparations are necessary. They include: cleaning the house, setting a festive table, cooking a festive meal, adorning the dining table with flowers, attending to personal grooming, and wearing apparel appropriate for Shabbat.
>
> Because Shabbat is not only a day of physical rest but of spiritual rejuvenation, it is important to allow time prior to the commencement of Shabbat to disengage from weekday concerns and create an atmosphere and mood conducive to the serenity of Shabbat. Wherever possible, all members of the household should be involved in Shabbat preparations.[46]

A-10 The *mitzvah* of hospitality (*Hachnasat Orechim*)

> It is a *mitzvah* to invite guests to join in the celebration of Shabbat.[47] Ideally, no one should have to observe Shab-

bat alone. Therefore, one should pay particular attention
to newcomers in the community and others who are alone.
While every Jew is obligated to celebrate Shabbat whether
at home or away, the joy of Shabbat is increased by joining
הַכְנָסַת   with others. The *mitzvah* is called *Hachnasat Orechim*, and
אוֹרְחִים   Jewish tradition includes it among those that merit eternal
reward (see *Gates of Mitzvah*, page 43, E-10).

A-11 The *mitzvah* of Tzedakah*

צְדָקָה   It is always a *mitzvah* to give *Tzedakah*.[48] Following the
example of Talmudic sages, the tradition has recognized
the final moments before Shabbat as one of the regular
opportunities to perform the *mitzvah*.[49] The placing of
money in a *Tzedakah* box just prior to lighting the Shabbat candles is an excellent way to observe this *mitzvah*
and to teach it to children (see *Gates of Mitzvah*, pages
39–40, E-5, and the essay "*Tzedakah*," pages 121–123).

A-12 The *mitzvah* of kindling Shabbat candles (*Hadlakat Hanerot*)

הַדְלָקַת   It is a *mitzvah* to begin the observance of Shabbat with
הַנֵּרוֹת   the kindling of Shabbat candles[50] followed by the recitation of the appropriate blessing:[51]

בָּרוּךְ אַתָּה, יְיָ אֱלֹהֵינוּ, מֶלֶךְ הָעוֹלָם, אֲשֶׁר קִדְּשָׁנוּ
בְּמִצְוֹתָיו וְצִוָּנוּ לְהַדְלִיק נֵר שֶׁל שַׁבָּת.

*Ba-ruch a-ta, A-do-nai E-lo-hei-nu, me-lech ha-o-
lam, a-sher ki-de-sha-nu be-mits-vo-tav ve-tsi-va-nu
le-had-lik ner shel Shab-bat.*

---

*Tzedakah is usually translated as charity, but the Jewish concept of *Tzedakah* is
much broader. The word is derived from *Tzedek*—righteousness or justice—and
the implication is that righteousness and justice require the *sharing* of one's sub-
stance with others because ultimately, "the earth is the Lord's" (Psalm 24:1) and
we are but stewards of whatever we possess.

Blessed is the Lord our God, Ruler of the universe, Who hallows us with His mitzvot and commands us to kindle the lights of Shabbat.

A complete ritual welcoming Shabbat can be found in *Gates of the House*, page 30. Tradition prescribes that the *mitzvah* of *Hadlakat Hanerot* is the privilege of the women of the household, but where there are no women a man should also perform it.[52]

The lighting of candles marks the formal beginning of Shabbat,[53] and as our liturgy suggests, the candles are a "symbol of the divine."[54] Therefore, the candles are kindled before the Shabbat meal in the room where the meal is to take place to indicate that they are lit only in honor of Shabbat—not as a table decoration but as a symbol of Shabbat holiness.

זָכוֹר
שָׁמוֹר

It is customary to light at least two candles[55] corresponding to the words *Zachor* ("Remember") and *Shamor* ("Observe") in the two versions of the Decalogue.[56] However, in some homes it is the custom to light one candle for each member of the household. The lighting of candles in the synagogue is not a substitute for performance of the *mitzvah* in the home.[57]

A-13 The *mitzvah* of *Kiddush*

קִדּוּשׁ

זִכָּרוֹן
לְמַעֲשֵׂה
בְּרֵאשִׁית

זֵכֶר לִיצִיאַת
מִצְרָיִם

It is a *mitzvah* to recite *Kiddush* over wine[58] at the Shabbat table. *Kiddush* is a blessing which proclaims the sanctity of Shabbat, thanks God for having given us Shabbat as an inheritance, and emphasizes the themes of Shabbat as a commemoration of Creation (*Zikaron lema-aseh vereshit*) and a memorial to the Exodus from Egypt (*Zecher liytsi-at Mitsrayim*). After the recitation of *Kiddush*, all present should drink the wine. In many households a *Kiddush* cup is provided for each participant. The text of *Kiddush* may be found in *Gates of Prayer*, page 719, and in *Gates of the House*, pages 33–34.

The recitation of *Kiddush* in the synagogue is not a substitute for the performance of the *mitzvah* in the home.[59]

A-14 The *mitzvah* of blessing children

It is a *mitzvah* for a parent or parents to bless child(ren) at the Shabbat table each week.[60] Families may establish their own ritual or use the traditional words:

FOR A BOY—

יְשִׂימְךָ אֱלֹהִים כְּאֶפְרַיִם וְכִמְנַשֶּׁה.

Ye-si-me-cha E-lo-him ke-Ef-ra-yim ve-chi-Me-na-sheh.

May God inspire you to live in the tradition of Ephraim and Menasheh, who carried forward the life of our people.

FOR A GIRL—

יְשִׂימֵךְ אֱלֹהִים כְּשָׂרָה, רִבְקָה, רָחֵל וְלֵאָה.

Ye-si-mech E-lo-him ke-Sa-ra, Riv-ka, Ra-chel, ve-Le-a.

May God inspire you to live in the tradition of Sarah and Rebekah, Rachel and Leah, who carried forward the life of our people.

יְבָרֶכְךָ יְיָ וְיִשְׁמְרֶךָ,
יָאֵר יְיָ פָּנָיו אֵלֶיךָ וִיחֻנֶּךָּ,
יִשָּׂא יְיָ פָּנָיו אֵלֶיךָ וְיָשֵׂם לְךָ שָׁלוֹם.
אָמֵן.

Ye-va-re-che-cha A-do-nai ve-yish-me-re-cha,
ya-er A-do-nai pa-nav e-lei-cha viy-chu-ne-ka,
yi-sa A-do-nai pa-nav e-lei-cha ve-ya-sem le-cha
shalom.
Amen.

The Lord bless you and keep you;
the Lord look kindly upon you and be gracious to you;
the Lord bestow His favor upon you and give you peace.
Amen.

Children may wish to respond to the blessing with words
of their own or with the following text:

הָרַחֲמָן הוּא יְבָרֵךְ אֶת אָבִי מוֹרִי בַּעַל הַבַּיִת הַזֶּה וְאֶת
אִמִּי מוֹרָתִי בַּעֲלַת הַבַּיִת הַזֶּה.

Ha-ra-cha-man hu ye-va-rech et a-vi mo-ri ba-al
ha-ba-yit ha-zeh ve-et i-mi mo-ra-ti ba-a-lat ha-ba-
yit ha-zeh.

Merciful God, bless my beloved father and mother who
guide our home and family.[61]

In addition, husband and wife should recite mutual words
of praise. They may wish to use their own words, portions
of Proverbs 31 (in praise of a woman), or portions of
Psalm 112 (in praise of a man) which may be found in
Gates of the House, pages 31–32.

A-15 The *mitzvah* of Hamotsi

הַמּוֹצִיא　　It is a *mitzvah* to recite *Hamotsi* at every meal.[62] The text
is as follows:

בָּרוּךְ אַתָּה, יְיָ אֱלֹהֵינוּ, מֶלֶךְ הָעוֹלָם, הַמּוֹצִיא לֶחֶם מִן
הָאָרֶץ.

*Ba-ruch a-ta, A-do-nai E-lo-hei-nu, me-lech
ha-o-lam, ha-mo-tsi le-chem min ha-a-rets.*

*Blessed is the Lord our God, Ruler of the universe, Who
causes bread to come forth from the earth.*

חַלָּה On Shabbat, it is recited over *Challah*, which is either cut
or broken and then eaten by all present. In some homes
it is customary to have two *Challot* on the Shabbat table.[63]
When the pieces of *Challah* are distributed, they are sprinkled with salt as a reminder that the table is a *Mizbeach*
מִזְבֵּחַ מְעַט *Me-at* (a miniature altar).[64]

A-16 The Shabbat table

The *mitzvah* of taking delight in Shabbat is appropriately
expressed at the Shabbat meal.[65] Special foods and bev-
erages should grace the table. Joy is enhanced by singing
זְמִירוֹת Shabbat songs (*Zemirot*) (see "For Further Reading," pages
199–200).

According to the Talmud, our conversation on Shabbat
should be different from that of the rest of the week.[66] In
keeping with the spirit of Shabbat, one might discuss the
weekly Torah portion or matters of concern to the Jewish
people. By focusing on those matters which increase our
awareness and sensitivity to general human and Jewish
values, our own humanity and Jewishness are heightened.
Conversation relating to business should be reserved for
other times.

A-17 The *mitzvah* of *Birkat Hamazon*

At the conclusion of all meals, and of course on Shabbat,
בִּרְכַּת הַמָּזוֹן it is a *mitzvah* to recite grace after meals (*Birkat Hamazon*).[67] The text may be found in *Gates of the House*, pages
6–10.

A-18 The *mitzvah* of congregational worship

> It is a *mitzvah* to join the congregation in worship on
> Shabbat.[68] As members of the Jewish people, we have
> personal and communal responsibilities. Participation in
> the congregational worship service is one such communal
> obligation, but our attendance at services goes beyond
> obligation. The public celebration of Shabbat through
> prayer, song, and Torah study is the heart of the Shabbat
> experience. Regular Shabbat worship draws us into the
> circle of community, strengthening our ties to one another
> and to the historical values that we as Jews hold dear. If
> illness prevents attendance at services, Shabbat prayers should
> be recited at home.

A-19 The Shabbat noon meal

> The noon meal provides additional opportunities for mak-
> ing Shabbat special. The *mitzvot* of *Kiddush*,[69] *Hamotsi*,
> and *Birkat Hamazon* should be observed, as well as the
> singing of *Zemirot*, as on Friday evening (see A-16 above).
> The texts may be found in *Gates of the House*, pages 6–18
> and 35–40. At the noon meal also, conversation should
> be in keeping with the spirit of Shabbat (see A-16 above).

A-20 The *mitzvah* of study (*Talmud Torah*)

תַּלְמוּד תּוֹרָה   It is a *mitzvah* to study Torah every day,[70] even more so
> on Shabbat.[71] The reading of the *Sidrah*, the weekly Torah
> selection, during the synagogue service should lead to fur-
> ther appropriate reading and related study.[72] By joining
> with family or friends to study on Shabbat, the joy of
> learning is increased and the observance of Shabbat is
> enriched by intellectual stimulation and companionship.
> On Shabbat afternoon, it is the custom to study the weekly
סִדְרָה   *Sidrah* as well as some other work of Jewish significance,
> i.e., traditional texts such as *Ethics of the Fathers* or con-
> temporary works which increase one's Jewish knowledge.

A-21 The *mitzvah* of visiting the sick (*Bikur Cholim*)

בִּקוּר חוֹלִים   It is a *mitzvah* to visit the ill and shut-ins at anytime.[73] By performing this *mitzvah* on Shabbat, one brings them a measure of Shabbat joy.

A-22 Weddings and wedding preparations

Weddings should not take place on Shabbat.[74] In making unavoidable final preparations for a Saturday evening wedding, care should be taken to perserve the spirit of Shabbat.

A-23 Mourning on Shabbat

שִׁבְעָה   Formal mourning (i.e., the observance of *Shiv-ah*) is interrupted for the observance of Shabbat. On Shabbat and festivals mourners should attend synagogue services and observe the *mitzvot* of that day[75] (see *Gates of Mitzvah*, page 60, D-3). Funerals are not held on Shabbat, nor do people visit the cemetery[76] (see *Gates of Mitzvah*, page 55, C-4).

A-24 Maintaining the special quality of Shabbat

One should maintain and enjoy the special quality of Shabbat throughout the entire day from the lighting of Shabbat candles until the recitation of *Havdalah* (see A-25). This may be done by choosing those activities which will complement and enrich one's spiritual life. Special care should be taken to conduct oneself in such a manner and to participate in such activities as will promote the distinctive Shabbat qualities of *Kedushah, Menuchah*, and *Oneg*.

A-25 The *mitzvah* of *Havdalah*

הַבְדָּלָה   At the conclusion of Shabbat, it is a *mitzvah* to recite *Havdalah*[77] separating the holy from the ordinary, Shabbat from the other days of the week. The *Havdalah* service includes four blessings:

בָּרוּךְ אַתָּה, יְיָ אֱלֹהֵינוּ, מֶלֶךְ הָעוֹלָם,
בּוֹרֵא פְּרִי הַגָּפֶן.

Over wine—*Ba-ruch a-ta, A-do-nai E-lo-hei-nu,*
me-lech ha-o-lam, bo-re pe-ri ha-ga-fen.

Blessed is the Lord our God, Ruler of the universe, Creator
of the fruit of the vine.

בָּרוּךְ אַתָּה, יְיָ אֱלֹהֵינוּ, מֶלֶךְ הָעוֹלָם,
בּוֹרֵא מִינֵי בְשָׂמִים.

Over spices—*Ba-ruch a-ta, A-do-nai E-lo-hei-nu,*
me-lech ha-o-lam, bo-re mi-nei
ve-sa-mim.

Blessed is the Lord our God, Ruler of the universe, Creator
of all the spices.

בָּרוּךְ אַתָּה, יְיָ אֱלֹהֵינוּ, מֶלֶךְ הָעוֹלָם,
בּוֹרֵא מְאוֹרֵי הָאֵשׁ.

Over light—*Ba-ruch a-ta, A-do-nai E-lo-hei-nu,*
me-lech ha-o-lam, bo-re me-o-rei ha-esh.

Blessed is the Lord our God, Ruler of the universe, Creator
of the light of fire.

בָּרוּךְ אַתָּה, יְיָ אֱלֹהֵינוּ, מֶלֶךְ הָעוֹלָם,
הַמַּבְדִּיל בֵּין קֹדֶשׁ לְחוֹל, בֵּין
אוֹר לְחֹשֶׁךְ, בֵּין יוֹם הַשְּׁבִיעִי לְשֵׁשֶׁת
יְמֵי הַמַּעֲשֶׂה. בָּרוּךְ אַתָּה, יְיָ, הַמַּבְדִּיל
בֵּין קֹדֶשׁ לְחוֹל.

Havdalah—*Ba-ruch a-ta, A-do-nai E-lo-hei-nu,*
me-lech ha-o-lam, ha-mav-dil bein
ko-desh le-chol, bein or le-cho-shech, bein
yom ha-she-vi-i le-she-shet ye-mei
ha-ma-a-seh.
Ba-ruch a-ta, A-do-nai, ha-mav-dil bein
ko-desh le-chol.

Blessed is the Lord our God, Ruler of the universe, Who
separates sacred from profane, light from darkness, the seventh
day of rest from the six days of labor.
Blessed is the Lord, Who separates the sacred from the pro-
fane.

A special multi-wicked braided candle is used,[78] which is
customarily held by the youngest person present. At the
conclusion of the service the participants wish each other
"*Shavua tov*" ("A good week").

The Days
of Awe

YAMIM NORA-IM

ROSH HASHANAH

In the seventh month, on the first day of the
month, you shall observe complete rest, a holy
day commemorated with loud blasts.

—LEVITICUS 23:24

In the seventh month, on the first day of the
month, you shall observe a holy day; you shall
not work at your occupations. You shall observe
it as a day when the horn is sounded.

—NUMBERS 29:1

On the first day of the seventh month, Ezra the
priest brought the Torah before the assembly,
both men and women and all who could
understand, and he read from it facing in front
of the Water Gate from early morning till noon.

—NEHEMIAH 8:2–3

ROSH Hashanah, which falls on the first of the Hebrew month of Tishri, marks the beginning of the new year.[79] It is, however, far more than the first day of the calendar year. It is the beginning of a ten-day period of rigorous self-examination which continues through Yom Kippur.[80] So important did the Rabbis consider this period, that they proclaimed the whole of the preceding month of Elul as a period of preparation.[81]

The Torah designates the first of Tishri as a day of "memorial, proclaimed with the blast of horns" (Leviticus 23:24, Numbers 29:1). For Jews the sound of the *Shofar* became a multi-faceted symbol recalling past events, looking to the Messianic future, proclaiming divine sovereignty—and much more.[82] The sound of the *Shofar* is a call to hearken to the divine summons, to examine our hearts, and to plead our case before the Eternal Judge.

Rabbinic tradition identifies Rosh Hashanah as *Yom Hadin*, Judgment Day, and in this spirit a Talmudic parable[83] pictures God as sitting in judgment of the world and each individual on Rosh Hashanah. The image of God as judge, about to inscribe human beings according to their deeds in the appropriate Book of Life, underscores the Jewish concept of human beings as moral free agents responsible for the choices which they make. We are further encouraged to believe that our fate, and indeed the fate of the entire world, depends upon our every act.[84]

Following from the theme of divine judgment is the concept of making amends for the past and beginning the year with a clean slate. According to Judaic tradition, "repentance, prayer, and charity (*Teshuvah, Tefilah*, and *Tzedakah*) temper judgment's severe decree."[85] Through these *mitzvot* Jews seek to re-establish their relationship with God and with other human beings and accomplish reconciliation with both.

The theme of Rosh Hashanah is that in spite of human weakness "the gates of repentance are always open."[86] The struggle for right-eousness never ceases. The *mitzvot* and customs of Rosh Hashanah are designed to help Jews enter into the new year with a new spirit so that they might be "inscribed in the Book of Life and Blessing."

A. ROSH HASHANAH

A-1 The month of Elul

אֱלוּל It is a *mitzvah* to prepare for the Days of Awe during the preceding month of Elul.[87] Special penitential prayers called

סְלִיחוֹת *Selichot* are added to the daily liturgy,[88] and many congregations have a late night *Selichot* service, usually on the Saturday night before Rosh Hashanah.[89] The text of the service may be found in *Gates of Forgiveness*. Some con-

שׁוֹפָר gregations follow the custom of blowing the *Shofar* each weekday during the month of Elul as a reminder of the approaching season of atonement.[90]

Since proper preparation includes serious reflection and self-examination, it is important to set aside regular periods of time for contemplation and study. The High Holy Day liturgy of *Gates of Repentance* and S. Y. Agnon's *Days of Awe* are particularly appropriate texts for study.

It is customary to visit the graves of relatives during the month of Elul and during the Ten Days of Repentance.[91] Through such visits, links to preceding generations are reinforced, and by contemplating the virtues of the deceased and their devotion to faith and people, we find strength. (An appropriate prayer to recite at the grave may be found in *Gates of the House*, page 217.)

A-2 The *mitzvah* of observing Rosh Hashanah

It is a *mitzvah* to observe Rosh Hashanah on the first of Tishri. As the Torah teaches, "In the seventh month, on the first day of the month, you shall observe a sacred occasion: You shall not work at your occupations. You shall observe it as a day when the *Shofar* is sounded" (Numbers 29:1).

A-3   The *mitzvah* of repentance (*Teshuvah*)

תְּשׁוּבָה

It is a *mitzvah* to express one's personal repentance (*Teshuvah*) on Rosh Hashanah.[92] According to the traditional symbolism, God sits in judgment of the world on Rosh Hashanah.[93] Through repentance (*Teshuvah*), prayer (*Tefilah*), and charity (*Tzedakah*), one begins moving towards reconciliation with God and other human beings. This process reaches its climax on Yom Kippur.

תְּפִלָּה

צְדָקָה

Repentance begins with the recognition of one's faults, failures, and weaknesses and the willingness to attempt to change and rectify impaired relationships. Through discussion with friends and family, one seeks understanding and forgiveness. The reciting of confessional prayers opens the heart to repentance. The goal of repentance is to turn (*lashuv*) the individual and the community toward each other and toward God.[94]

לָשׁוּב

A-4   The *mitzvah* of *Tzedakah*

צְדָקָה

It is always a *mitzvah* to give *Tzedakah*, but on Rosh Hashanah, this *mitzvah* takes on added significance.[95] *Tzedakah* is one of the *mitzvot* which tempers judgment's "severe decree." Through direct aid to the needy and to the institutions which serve the needy and through aid to synagogues and other institutions which support the spiritual and cultural life of the Jewish community, we exemplify our obligation as human beings to share the bounty of the earth with others. The period immediately before Rosh Hashanah is an especially appropriate time to fulfill this *mitzvah*.

In many homes, it is the custom to deposit money in the *Tzedakah* box as one comes to the table for the lighting of the candles before the festive meal.

A-5   The *mitzvot* of the Holy Day

Shabbat observance is the model for the observance of Rosh Hashanah and all other major festivals.[96] The following *mitzvot* are common to both Shabbat and Rosh Hashanah: (1) Preparation (see "Shabbat," A-9); (2) including guests at the festive table (see "Shabbat," A-10); (3) lighting candles (see "Shabbat," A-12); (4) *Kiddush* (see "Shabbat," A-13); (5) blessing children (see "Shabbat," A-14); (6) *Hamotsi* (see "Shabbat," A-15)[97]; and (7) grace after meals (see "Shabbat," A-17). Some of the blessings and prayers differ from those on Shabbat. The text may be found in *Gates of the House*, pages 6-18, 41-48.

קִדּוּשׁ

הַמּוֹצִיא

A-6   Apples and honey

It is customary to dip a piece of apple in honey and to eat it after reciting the appropriate blessing. The apple and honey symbolize the hope for a good and sweet year. The text of the prayer is as follows:

יְהִי רָצוֹן מִלְּפָנֶיךָ, יְיָ אֱלֹהֵינוּ וֵאלֹהֵי אֲבוֹתֵינוּ,
שֶׁתְּחַדֵּשׁ עָלֵינוּ שָׁנָה טוֹבָה וּמְתָקָה.

*Ye-hi ra-tson mi-le-fa-nei-cha, A-do-nai E-lo-hei-nu
ve-lo-hei a-vo-tei-nu, she-te-cha-desh a-lei-nu sha-na
to-va u-me-tu-ka.*

*Lord our God and God of our people, may the new year be
good and sweet for us.*

בָּרוּךְ אַתָּה, יְיָ אֱלֹהֵינוּ, מֶלֶךְ הָעוֹלָם, בּוֹרֵא פְּרִי הָעֵץ.

*Ba-ruch a-ta, A-do-nai E-lo-hei-nu, me-lech ha-o-lam,
bo-re pe-ri ha-ets.*

*Blessed are You, O Lord our God, Ruler of the Universe,
creator of the fruit of the tree.*

A-7   The *mitzvah* of congregational worship

It is a *mitzvah* to join the congregation in worship on Rosh Hashanah.[98] As members of the Jewish people, we have personal and communal responsibilities. Participation in the congregational worship service is one such communal obligation, but our attendance at services goes beyond obligation. The public celebration of Rosh Hashanah through prayer, song, and Torah study is the heart of the Rosh Hashanah experience. Rosh Hashanah worship draws us into the circle of the community, strengthening our ties to one another and to the historical values that we Jews hold dear. If illness prevents attendance at services, Rosh Hashanah prayers should be recited at home.

For a discussion of the special features of the services and the Torah and *Haftarah* selections, see "Fragments of Faith: On Holy Day Liturgy," pages 147–153, and "Torah and *Haftarah* Readings," pages 155–159.

A-8   The *mitzvah* of hearing the *Shofar*

שׁוֹפָר

It is a *mitzvah* to hear the sound of the *Shofar* on Rosh Hashanah, as the Torah teaches, "You shall observe it as a day when the horn is sounded" (Numbers 29:1).[99] Jewish tradition is rich with explanations for the meaning of the *Shofar*.[100] The liturgy of the *Shofar* service emphasizes the themes of God's sovereignty (*Malchuyot*), reminiscences of encounters between God and Israel (*Zichronot*), and God's promise of redemption (*Shofarot*) (see "Fragments of Faith: On Holy Day Liturgy," pages 147–153, and *Gates of Repentance*, pages 138–151). As the *Shofar* is sounded, one should concentrate on its meaning and hearken to its call.[101] Provisions should be made so that those unable to attend the synagogue because of illness or infirmity may hear the sound of the *Shofar*.

מַלְכֻיּוֹת
זִכְרוֹנוֹת
שׁוֹפָרוֹת

A-9   The *mitzvah* of refraining from work on Rosh Hashanah

It is a *mitzvah* to refrain from work on Rosh Hashanah. As the Torah teaches, "In the seventh month, on the first day of the month, you shall observe complete rest" (Leviticus 23:23). (See also "Shabbat," A-5, page 22). Chil-

dren and university students should not attend classes, and
all who are able should attend synagogue services.

A-10 Greetings on Rosh Hashanah

It is a time-honored tradition to greet friends and neigh-
bors during the Days of Awe, especially on Rosh Hashanah, by expressing the wish that they be blessed
with a good year. The traditional words of blessing,
whether uttered personally or sent through the mail, are
" לְשָׁנָה טוֹבָה תִּכָּתֵבוּ ," *"Le-sha-na to-va ti-ka-te-vu"*
("May you be inscribed [in the Book of Life] for a
good year"). After Rosh Hashanah one might say
" גְּמַר חֲתִימָה טוֹבָה ," *"Ge-mar cha-ti-ma to-va"* ("May
the final decree be good"); or " לְשָׁנָה טוֹבָה תֵּחָתֵמוּ ,"
"Le-sha-na to-va te-cha-te-mu" ("May you be sealed [in
the Book of Life] for a good year").

A-11 Visiting with friends and relatives

On Rosh Hashanah it is customary to visit with friends
and relatives, to wish them well. Such visits are part of
שִׂמְחָה the joy (*Simchah*) of the festival.

A-12 The Second Day of Rosh Hashanah

Although Reform Judaism has adopted the calendar of
the Torah observing Rosh Hashanah for only one day
(Leviticus 23:24 and Numbers 29:21), there are some
congregations that have adopted the custom of the Land
of Israel observing Rosh Hashanah for two days (see "The
Jewish Calendar," pages 7–11).

A-13 Mourning on Rosh Hashanah

שִׁבְעָה Formal mourning (i.e., the observance of *Shiv-ah*) is suspended for the observance of Rosh Hashanah, at which
time the mourners should attend services and observe the
customs of the day (see "Shabbat," A-23, page 31). Tra-

dition prescribes the complete termination of formal mourning when a festival intervenes.[102] While Reform Judaism agrees to the suspension of formal mourning for the holy day itself, it is left to the family to decide whether or not to resume *Shiv-ah* after a festival, particularly when the festival falls within a day or two of the death (*Gates of Mitzvah*, "Death and Mourning," page 60, D-3).

A-14 The *mitzvah* of *Havdalah*

הַבְדָּלָה

At the conclusion of Rosh Hashanah it is a *mitzvah* to recite *Havdalah* prayers separating the holy from the ordinary—Rosh Hashanah from the other days of the year.[103] The text of *Havdalah* may be found in *Gates of the House*, page 71.

THE ten-day period from Rosh Hashanah through Yom Kippur is known as *Aseret Yemei Teshuvah*, the Ten Days of Repentance.[104] On Rosh Hashanah the Jew takes the first steps toward atonement. But this initial recognition of sin with its accompanying remorse requires further steps to complete the process of repentance.[105]

Activities during this period should be directed toward the sacred goal of reconciliation with both God and other human beings. Jewish tradition teaches that Yom Kippur makes atonement only for those sins which we commit against God, but it does not atone for those sins which we commit against other human beings unless we first attempt to make amends and seek their forgiveness.[106]

The mood of Rosh Hashanah and Yom Kippur permeates these days. A high point during this period is *Shabbat Shuvah*, the Sabbath of Return. Turning toward God and toward other people is the purpose of these days.

B. ASERET YEMEI TESHUVAH
(TEN DAYS OF REPENTANCE)

B-1   The *mitzvah* of self-examination

> It is a *mitzvah* to reflect upon our behavior during the ten-day period beginning with Rosh Hashanah and concluding with Yom Kippur, and to determine how to improve ourselves in the new year.[107] During these intervening days one should set aside a period each day for reflection and self-examination.

B-2   The *mitzvah* of reconciliation

> It is a *mitzvah* to seek reconciliation during the Ten Days
> of Repentance with those whom one may have hurt or
> harmed during the past year. Our tradition teaches, "For
> transgressions against God, the Day of Atonement atones;
> but for transgressions of one human being against another,
> the Day of Atonement does not atone until they have
> made peace with one another."[108] It is appropriate to ap-
> proach any person whom we might have offended in order
> to bring about reconciliation.

B-3   The *mitzvah* of forgiveness

> It is a *mitzvah* to forgive a person who has wronged you
> during the past year and who seeks your forgiveness.[109]
> The Talmud states: "A person should be as pliant as a
> reed and not hard like a cedar in granting forgiveness."[110]
> Bearing a grudge is destructive to both parties and subverts
> the purposes of the Ten Days of Repentance.

B-4   Visiting graves of relatives

> Many observe the custom of visiting the graves of relatives
> during this period and of reciting prayers in their mem-
> ory.[111] Texts of appropriate prayers may be found in *Gates
> of the House*, page 217.

B-5   *Shabbat Shuvah*

שַׁבַּת שׁוּבָה
הַפְטָרָה
שׁוּבָה יִשְׂרָאֵל

> The Shabbat between Rosh Hashanah and Yom Kippur
> is known as *Shabbat Shuvah*. Its name is derived from the
> first word of the *Haftarah*, Hosea 14:2–10, which begins
> with the words "*Shuvah Yisra-el*, Return O Israel." One
> should make a special effort to attend *Shabbat Shuvah*
> services in order to hear the reading of this *Haftarah* as
> an introspective prelude to Yom Kippur.

ON THIS DAY LIFE AND DEATH SHALL BE WRITTEN IN THE BOOK OF REMEMBRANCE

היום יכתב בספר הזכרונות החיים והמת

YOM KIPPUR

For on this day atonement shall be made for you
to cleanse you of all your sins; you shall be clean.
It shall be a sabbath of complete rest for you
and you shall practice self-denial; it is a law for
all time.

—LEVITICUS 16:30–31

Mark, the tenth day of this seventh month is the
Day of Atonement. . . . For it is the Day of
Atonement on which expiation is made on your
behalf before the Lord your God. . . . Do no
work whatever; it is a law for all time,
throughout the generations in your settlements. It
shall be a sabbath of complete rest for you and
you shall practice self-denial; on the ninth day of
the month at evening from evening to evening,
you shall observe this your sabbath.

—LEVITICUS 23:27–28,31–32

On the tenth day of the same seventh month you
shall observe a sacred occasion when you shall
practice self-denial.

—NUMBERS 29:7

YOM Kippur, the Day of Atonement, occurs on the tenth of Tishri (Leviticus 23:27). It is the culmination of the Ten Days of Repentance. It alone of all the Jewish holidays is the equivalent of Shabbat in sanctity.[112] Its mood is reflective and introspective—a day devoted totally to self-examination, confession, and atonement.

Yom Kippur provides us with the opportunity to alter our conduct, readjust our values, and set things right in our lives. The day demands absolute honesty as we confess our wrongdoings: "We have sinned, we have transgressed, we have done perversely."[113] The grandeur of the liturgy and music adds to the drama and seriousness of the day. From *Kol Nidrei*, the eve of Yom Kippur, to the last triumphant note of the *Shofar* at the conclusion of the *Ne-ilah*, its purpose is to move us toward reconciliation with God and our fellow human beings.

Primary among the *mitzvot* leading to atonement is fasting. The Torah says three times, "And this shall be to you a law for all times! In the seventh month, on the tenth day of the month you shall practice self-denial" (Leviticus 16:29 and 23:27; Numbers 29:7). Tradition interprets "self-denial" as fasting, and the threefold repetition of this *mitzvah* in the Torah has suggested three reasons for fasting as described in our prayerbook.

reasons for fasting

Judaism calls for self-discipline. When we control our appetites on Yom Kippur, we remember that on other days, too, we can be masters, not slaves, of our desires.

Judaism calls for empathy. When we consciously experience hunger, we are more likely to consider millions who need no Yom Kippur in order to suffer hunger. For some, most days are days without food enough for themselves and their children.

Judaism calls for penitence. The confession we make with our lips is
a beginning. The penance we inflict upon our bodies through fasting,
leads us along further still toward the acknowledgment that we have
sinned against ourselves and others.

(Gates of Repentance, page 229)

Yom Kippur is a day of concentration on the past so that the
future may be better for us as individuals, better for us as a community, and better for us as part of the human community. Despite
its solemnity, Yom Kippur is also a day of joy, when the truly penitent
person begins gradually to feel at one with God and humankind.
Reconcilitation is the goal of the day's prayers and fast. When the
final blast of the *Shofar* is heard at the end of *Ne-ilah*, those who
have observed the day with sincerity should feel that they have been
inscribed and sealed in the Book of Life.

C.   YOM KIPPUR

C-1   The *mitzvah* of observing Yom Kippur

It is a *mitzvah* to observe Yom Kippur on the tenth of
the Hebrew month of Tishri. As the Torah says, "Mark
the tenth day of this seventh month as the Day of Atonement. It shall be a sacred occasion for you. . . . For it is
the Day of Atonement, on which expiation is made on
your behalf before the Lord your God" (Leviticus 23:27–28).

C-2   The *mitzvah* of repentance (*Teshuvah*)

It is a *mitzvah* to repent on Yom Kippur.[114] As the intense
ten-day period of self-examination, reflection, and reconciliation initiated on Rosh Hashanah reaches its climax,
the recitation of confessional prayers brings into sharp focus
our shortcomings and failures which alienate us from God.

תְּשׁוּבָה   It is through repentance (*Teshuvah*) that we return to God
and find God returning to us.[115]

C-3   The *mitzvah* of reconciliation

> It is a *mitzvah* for each person to seek reconciliation with members of his or her family and with all those one might have offended before the onset of Yom Kippur.[116] One should not enter into the sacred day of reconciliation without having made every effort at personal reconciliation.

C-4   The *mitzvah* of *Tzedakah*

צְדָקָה
תְּפִלָּה
תְּשׁוּבָה

> It is always a *mitzvah* to give *Tzedakah*.[117] However, *Tzedakah* (charity)—along with *Tefilah* (prayer) and *Teshuvah* (repentance)—is an integral part of Yom Kippur observance.

כַּפָּרָה

> There is an old custom of setting aside money (referred to as *Kaparah*, atonement money) before sunset on the eve of Yom Kippur. Implicit in this act of *Kaparah* is the idea that this charity money serves as an atonement for one's sins.[118]

> Therefore, it is especially appropriate before the onset of the day to perform specific acts of *Tzedakah* which will improve the spiritual and/or material well-being of the community.

C-5   The meal on Erev Yom Kippur

> Unlike the meal held on the eves of Sabbaths and other festivals, there are no special rituals connected with the Erev Yom Kippur meal, because it is eaten before the

הַמּוֹצִיא
בִּרְכַּת הַמָּזוֹן
סְעֻדָּה
מַפְסֶקֶת

> sacred day begins. The *mitzvot* of *Hamotsi* and *Birkat Hamazon* should be observed as at any meal. This meal, which is called *Se-udah Mafseket* (the concluding meal before a fast), should begin early so that it is completed before the onset of the Holy Day.[119]

> It should be noted that *Kiddush* is not recited at this meal, which must be completed before the onset of Yom Kippur. Since the *Kiddush* usually sets aside the festival

as holy and may not be recited before the beginning of
the festival, and since the *Kiddush* is normally recited over
either wine or bread (neither of which may be consumed
on Yom Kippur), *Kiddush* may not be recited at the *Se-
udah Mafseket.*

C-6   The *mitzvah* of kindling Yom Kippur lights

It is a *mitzvah* to light and recite the appropriate blessing
over the Yom Kippur lights after the meal and before
leaving for the synagogue.[120]

בָּרוּךְ אַתָּה, יְיָ אֱלֹהֵינוּ, מֶלֶךְ הָעוֹלָם, אֲשֶׁר קִדְּשָׁנוּ בְּמִצְוֹתָיו,
וְצִוָּנוּ לְהַדְלִיק נֵר שֶׁל יוֹם הַכִּפּוּרִים.

Ba-ruch a-ta, A-do-nai E-lo-hei-nu, me-lech ha-o-
lam, a-sher ki-de-sha-nu be-mits-vo-tav ve-tsi-va-nu
le-had-lik ner shel Yom Ha-ki-pu-rim.

*Blessed is the Lord our God, Ruler of the Universe, by Whose
mitzvot we are hallowed, Who commands us to kindle the
lights of the Day of Atonement.*

The text of additional prayers may be found in *Gates of
the House*, page 56.

Unlike on Shabbat and the other festivals, Yom Kippur
candles are lit *after* the meal, because the lighting of the
candles marks the formal beginning of Yom Kippur and
therefore the beginning of the fast. Before lighting the
Yom Kippur candles, it is customary to light a memorial
candle, which will burn throughout the Holy Day. A single
candle may be used for all who are to be remembered.

C-7   The *mitzvah* of blessing children

It is a *mitzvah* for parents to bless their children before
leaving for the synagogue. Families may establish their

own ritual or use the traditional words (see "Shabbat," A-14, page 27, or *Gates of the House*, page 57).

C-8   The *mitzvah* of fasting

It is a *mitzvah* to fast throughout Yom Kippur.[121] The Torah (Leviticus 16:27 and 23:27) designates Yom Kippur as a day of self-denial or, more literally, affliction of the soul. Fasting requires self-discipline and is an attempt to control one's physical needs in order to concentrate on the spiritual. By symbolically denying the most basic biological necessity which humans share with all animals, we focus on that aspect of human nature which we share with God (see "Fasting on Yom Kippur," pages 146–147).

בַּר מִצְוָה
בַּת מִצְוָה

Children below the age of Bar/Bat Mitzvah should be taught to fast by beginning with a few hours' fast and increasing it each year until at thirteen they fast throughout Yom Kippur.[122] A person who is ill or pregnant should follow the advice of a physician on fasting.[123]

שׁוֹפָר
נְעִילָה

The fast begins with the kindling of Yom Kippur candles and concludes with the sounding of the *Shofar* at the end of *Ne-ilah*.

C-9   The *mitzvah* of congregational worship

כָּל נִדְרֵי
שׁוֹפָר
נְעִילָה

It is a *mitzvah* to join the congregation in worship by attending the *Kol Nidrei* service on Yom Kippur night and the several services on Yom Kippur day until the sounding of the *Shofar* at the end of *Ne-ilah*.[124] As members of the Jewish people, we have personal and communal responsibilities. Participation in the congregational worship service is one such communal obligation, but our attendance at services goes beyond obligation. The public celebration of Yom Kippur through prayer, song, and Torah study is the heart of the Yom Kippur experience. Yom Kippur worship draws us into the circle of the community, strengthening our ties to one another and to the historical values that we Jews hold dear. If illness prevents attendance at services, Yom Kippur prayers should be recited at home.

For a discussion of the special features of the services and the Torah and *Haftarah* selections, see "Fragments of Faith: On Holy Day Liturgy," pages 147–153, and "Torah and *Haftarah* Readings," pages 155–159.

C-10 The *mitzvah* of *Yizkor* (Memorial Service)

יִזְכֹּר   It is a *mitzvah* for every Jew to recite *Yizkor* on Yom Kippur.[125] Everyone should remain for *Yizkor* even if one's parents are alive, since *Yizkor* is a service of remembrance for the martyrs of our people as well as for our own relatives and friends (see *Gates of Mitzvah*, page 63, D-10, and "*Yizkor*," pages 153–155).

C-11 The *mitzvah* of refraining from work

It is a *mitzvah* to refrain from work on Yom Kippur. As the Torah states, "You shall do no work throughout that day. . . . It shall be a Shabbat of complete rest for you" (Leviticus 23:28, 32). The same strictures which apply to Shabbat apply to Yom Kippur which is known as the Sabbath of Sabbaths (see "Shabbat," A-5, page 22).

C-12 The *mitzvah* of *Havdalah*

הַבְדָּלָה   At the conclusion of Yom Kippur it is a *mitzvah* to recite *Havdalah* separating the holy from the ordinary, separating Yom Kippur from the other days of the year.[126] The text of *Havdalah* may be found in *Gates of Repentance*, pages 526–528, and in *Gates of the House*, pages 72–74.

C-13 Beginning the *Sukkah* after Yom Kippur

סֻכָּה   Immediately after *Havdalah*, it is customary to make a symbolic start on the *Sukkah,* i.e., by putting up one board or driving one nail.[127] In this manner one concludes the Ten Days of Repentance and turns at once to the performance of a *mitzvah*.

C-14 Breaking the fast

The meal following Yom Kippur should be a particularly joyous one. There is a feeling of exhilaration and relief which comes from having experienced a day of introspection and prayer in addition to a sense of Divine forgiveness. "Go your way, and eat your food with joy, and drink your wine, for God has already accepted your deeds."[128] It is especially appropriate to seek out those in the synagogue who are alone and invite them to join in breaking the fast.

שָׁלֹשׁ
רְגָלִים

The Pilgrimage Festivals

SHALOSH REGALIM

THE PILGRIMAGE FESTIVALS

Three times a year you shall hold a festival for Me. You shall observe the Feast of Unleavened Bread—eating unleavened bread for seven days as I have commanded you—at the set time in the month of Aviv, for in it you went forth from Egypt; and the Feast of the Harvest, of the first fruits of your work, of what you sow in the field; and the Feast of Ingathering at the end of the year when you gather in the results of your work from the field.

—EXODUS 23:14–16

Three times a year—on the Feast of Unleavened Bread, on the Feast of Weeks and on the Feast of Booths—all your males shall appear before the Lord your God in the place that He will choose.

—DEUTERONOMY 16:16

Then Solomon offered up burnt offerings to the Lord upon the altar . . . as the duty of each day required . . . and the annual feasts—the Feast of Unleavened Bread, the Feast of Weeks, and the Feast of Booths.

—II CHRONICLES 8:12–13

PESACH, Shavuot, and Sukkot are collectively known as the *Shalosh Regalim*, the Three Pilgrimage Festivals. During the existence of the Temple, they were the three annual occasions for pilgrimage to Jerusalem with offerings of thanksgiving for the bountiful harvest (Exodus 23:14). The eighth day of Sukkot, Atseret/Simchat Torah, while a separate festival[129] is considered part of the Sukkot holiday. While the origins of the Festivals are bound up with the seasonal changes and the agricultural cycle of ancient Israel, each also commemorates an important event in the history of the Jewish people: Pesach—the Exodus from Egypt; Shavuot—the giving of commandments at Mt. Sinai; and Sukkot—the forty-year journey through the wilderness. Through these historical associations the Festivals have remained significant in the life of the Jewish people even when they lived in the Diaspora, far from the land and its natural rhythms. Wherever Jews live they are able to celebrate liberation, revelation, and the journey towards the promised future.

The dates for celebrating the Festivals depend on the seasons as they occur in the Land of Israel. Thus, through the celebration of the Festivals, Jews, no matter where they live, feel a connection to the Land of Israel. The re-establishment of the State of Israel has helped renew the original agricultural significance of these Festivals for Jews throughout the world.

Rejoicing is characteristic of these Festivals, for they are opportunities to enrich our lives by renewing our commitment to the Judaic ideals of redemption, responsibility, and hope. Through the performance of the unique *mitzvot* of these Festivals, we participate in the continuing drama of sacred history, and through our celebration reaffirm our identity as part of the Jewish people.

The Festivals have certain *mitzvot* in common, and others which are unique to each Festival. For the sake of clarity, the *mitzvot* common to all Festivals are listed first in a preliminary section, followed by the *mitzvot* of the particular Festival.

A. THE PILGRIMAGE FESTIVALS

A-1   The *mitzvah* of observing the Festivals

> It is a *mitzvah* to observe the Festivals, as the Torah says, "Three times a year you shall hold a festival for Me" (Exodus 23:14). The Festivals are Pesach, Shavuot, and Sukkot (including Atseret/Simchat Torah).

A-2   The *mitzvah* of rejoicing (*Simchah*) on the Festivals

שִׂמְחָה
> It is a *mitzvah* to rejoice on the Festivals. The Torah teaches, "You shall rejoice in your festival" (Deuteronomy 16:14). This *mitzvah* sets the tone and mood of the Festivals.[130] Special liturgy, special ceremonial objects, and special foods make each celebration distinctive. Our joy is also derived from our recalling the decisive moments of the Jewish people which helped shape the ideals of Judaism. Through the reaffirmation of our commitment to those ideals and by joining together with other Jews in the ongoing task

תִּקּוּן עוֹלָם
> of perfecting the world (*Tikun Olam*), our lives take on renewed significance.

A-3   The *mitzvah* of the Festivals

> Shabbat observance provides the paradigm for the observance of the Festivals.[131] The following *mitzvot* are common to both Shabbat and the Festivals: (1) Preparation (see "Shabbat," A-9); (2) including guests at the festive table (see "Shabbat," A-10); (3) lighting candles (see "Shabbat," A-12); (4) *Kiddush* (see "Shabbat," A-13); (5)

הַמּוֹצִיא
בִּרְכַּת הַמָּזוֹן
> blessing of children (see "Shabbat," A-14); (6) *Hamotsi* (see "Shabbat," A-15); and (7) concluding the meal with

the *Birkat Hamazon* (see "Shabbat," A-17). Several of the blessings for the Festivals differ from those for Shabbat. The text of these prayers may be found in *Gates of the House*, pages 6–18, 41–48.

The mealtime conversation should reflect the joy and holiness of the occasion and should be interspersed with זְמִירוֹת *Zemirot* (table songs). The Festival table is a particularly appropriate place to discuss the meaning of the Festival.

A-4   The *mitzvah* of resting and avoiding work on the Festivals

It is a *mitzvah* to rest and abstain from work on the Festivals:[132] on the first and seventh day of Pesach (Leviticus 23:7, 8), on Shavuot (Leviticus 28:21), on the first day of Sukkot (Leviticus 23:35), and on Atseret/Simchat Torah (Leviticus 23:36). (See also "Shabbat," A-5, page 22). Since the Festivals are set aside for sanctification, one should refrain from those activities which do not contribute to the spirit of holiness. Just as adults should refrain from work, so children and university students should not attend classes but should instead participate in worship services.

A-5   The *mitzvah* of congregational worship

It is a *mitzvah* to join the congregation in worship on the Festivals:[133] on the first and seventh day of Pesach, on Shavuot, on the first day of Sukkot, and on Atseret/Simchat Torah. Through the worship service, every Jew shares the concerns of the community, strengthening the community through his or her participation. Each service has unique features which emphasize the special themes of the Festivals (see "Fragments of Faith: On Holy Day Liturgy," pages 147–153, and "Torah and *Haftarah* Readings," pages 155–159).

A-6   Mourning on the Festivals

שִׁבְעָה   Formal mourning (i.e., the observance of *Shiv-ah*) is suspended for the observance of the Festivals, at which time the mourners should attend services and observe the customs of the day[134] (see "Shabbat," A-23, page 31). Tradition prescribes the complete termination of *Shiv-ah* when a Festival intervenes. While Reform Judaism agrees to the suspension of formal mourning for the holy day itself, it is left to the family to decide whether or not to resume *Shiv-ah* after a Festival, particularly when it falls within a day or two of the death. If death occurs during the intermediate days of a Festival (i.e., *Chol Hamo-ed* of Pesach or Sukkot), the Rabbi should be consulted about the mourning period (see *Gates of Mitzvah*, page 60, D-3).

חוֹל הַמּוֹעֵד

A-7 Weddings on the Festivals

Jewish tradition has set aside Shabbat and the major festivals[135] as days on which weddings may not be held (see *Gates of Mitzvah*, pages 31–32, B-2, and "Shabbat," A-22, page 31).

A-8 The *mitzvah* of *Havdalah*

הַבְדָּלָה It is a *mitzvah* to recite *Havdalah* at the conclusion of the Festivals.[136] The blessing of separation is recited over wine and marks the end of the Festivals. The text may be found in *Gates of the House*, page 71. As the formal beginning of a Festival is marked by blessings and the Festival set apart and distinguished from ordinary days, the departure of the Festival is similarly marked. Having both a formal beginning and formal conclusion helps us to hallow the Festival and to savor the experience of the Festival even after it is concluded.

THREE TIMES
A YEAR YOU
SHALL HOLD
A FESTIVAL
FOR ME

שלש
רגלים
תחג
לי

PESACH

You shall observe the Feast of Unleavened Bread,
for on this very day I brought your ranks out of
the land of Egypt; you shall observe this day
throughout the generations as an institution for
all time. In the first month, from the fourteenth
day of the month at evening, you shall eat
unleavened bread until the twenty-first day of the
month at evening.

—EXODUS 12:17–18

You shall observe this as an institution for all
time, for you and your descendents. . . . And
when your children ask you, "What do you mean
by this rite?" You shall say, "It is the passover
sacrifice to the Lord, because God passed over
the houses of the Israelites in Egypt and smote
the Egyptians, but saved our houses."

—EXODUS 12:24, 26–27

You shall observe the Feast of Unleavened
Bread—eating unleavened bread for seven days as
I have commanded you—at the set time of the
month of Aviv, for in the month of Aviv you
went forth from Egypt.

—EXODUS 34:18

PESACH, which begins on the fifteenth of the Hebrew month of Nisan and lasts for seven days, commemorates the Exodus from Egypt.[137] In the Torah it is designated by several names, *Chag Haaviv* (Deuteronomy 16:1), the Spring Festival; *Chag Hamatzot* (Exodus 12:20), the Festival of Unleavened Bread; and *Chag Hapesach* (Exodus 12:17), the Festival of the Paschal Lamb. Current Pesach observance is a unique blend drawn from the agricultural and pastoral origins of the festival as well as from a seminal event in Jewish history.[138]

The liberation of the Jewish people from Egyptian bondage has become a powerful symbol of redemption—not only the redemption of the Jewish people but the redemption of the entire world. The *Haggadah*, reflecting the historic experience of the Jewish people, recognizes that slavery is not limited to physical bondage, but that spiritual slavery and social degradation are no less potent methods of depriving human beings of liberty.[139]

The highlight of Pesach observance is the *Seder* with its many symbolic foods and its elaborate liturgy, the *Haggadah*. The *Seder* is designed to recreate the events of redemption:

> In every generation, each of us should feel as though we ourselves had gone forth from Egypt, as it is written: "And you shall explain to your child on that day, it is because of what the Eternal did for me when I, *myself*, went forth from Egypt."[140]

As "*zeman cherutenu*," the season of our liberation, Pesach is a constant reminder of our responsibility to those who are oppressed or enslaved physically, intellectually, or ideologically. On Pesach we express our solidarity with other members of the Jewish community who are unable to celebrate Passover in freedom. The experience of redemption in the Passover celebration should inspire all Jews to assist in the future redemption of humanity. As the Midrash teaches, just as the Red Sea did not split until the Israelites stepped into it, so redemption cannot come unless we take the first step.[141]

B. PESACH

B-1 The *mitzvah* of observing Pesach

פֶּסַח It is a *mitzvah* to observe Pesach for seven days, beginning on the eve of the fifteenth of Nisan. As the Torah says, "In the first month, from the fourteenth day of the month at evening,[142] you shall eat unleavened bread until the twenty-first day of the month at evening" (Exodus 12:18).

B-2 The *mitzvah* of removing leaven (*Chamets*)

חָמֵץ It is a *mitzvah* to remove leaven from one's home prior to the beginning of Pesach. Leaven refers to products made from wheat, barley, rye, oats, and spelt, which have been permitted to leaven.[143] Ashkenazi custom adds rice, millet, corn, and legumes (like peas, beans, etc.) The removal of leaven is based on the Biblical injunction found in Exodus 12:15: "On the very first day you shall remove leaven from your house." If one does not actually remove all the leaven from one's home, one should place it in a closet or cabinet appropriately marked so that it will not be used during Pesach.[144]

בְּדִיקַת חָמֵץ Searching for leaven (*Bedikat Chamets*) on the night before the first *Seder* is a Pesach custom that has special appeal for children.[145] After the house has been cleaned for Pesach, a symbolic search for the last remains of leaven is made. At various places in the home, pieces of leaven are hidden. Then children, with flashlights or other illumination, search them out in the dark. The bread is gathered in a bag and burned or disposed of the next morning with the following blessing:

בָּרוּךְ אַתָּה, יְיָ אֱלֹהֵינוּ, מֶלֶךְ הָעוֹלָם, אֲשֶׁר קִדְּשָׁנוּ בְּמִצְוֹתָיו
וְצִוָּנוּ עַל בִּעוּר חָמֵץ.

Ba-ruch a-ta, A-do-nai E-lo-hei-nu, me-lech ha-o-
lam, a-sher ki-de-sha-nu be-mitz-vo-tav ve-tsi-va-nu
al bi-ur cha-mets.

*Blessed are you, O Lord our God, Ruler of the Universe, Who
hallows us with mitzvot and commands us to burn Chamets.*

מַצָּה

Since leaven has been removed, one should not eat bread
after breakfast on the day before the *Seder.* To heighten
the appetite for *Matzah* at the *Seder* itself, *Matzah* is not
eaten at least a full day before the *Seder.*[146]

B-3   The *mitzvah* of abstaining from eating leaven (*Chamets*)

חָמֵץ

It is a *mitzvah* to abstain from eating leaven (*Chamets*)
during the entire seven days of Pesach. As the Torah states,
"You shall eat nothing leavened . . ." (Exodus 12:20). Among
Reform Jews, abstaining from leaven may take many
forms—from not eating those foods which obviously contain leaven, such as bread or cake, to the more stringent
avoidance and examination of all ingredients in a particular
foodstuff. By consciously making a choice to abstain during the whole week of Pesach, one is constantly aware of
the Festival and one's identity as a Jew.

B-4   The *mitzvah* of preparing a *Seder*

סֵדֶר

הַגָּדָה

It is a *mitzvah* for everyone to participate in the preparations for the *Seder*—cooking, cleaning, and setting the
festive table.[147] The leader of the *Seder* has the special
obligation to review the *Haggadah* in advance and decide
which passages will be included. The experience of the
Seder is enhanced when all the participants are provided

with the same *Haggadah*.* In addition, the tradition encourages the use of beautiful ritual items to increase our enjoyment of the *mitzvot* (see "*Hidur Mitzvah*: The Aesthetics of *Mitzvot*," pages 162–164).

Although Reform Jews do not celebrate the second day of Pesach as a holiday, many people have a second *Seder*. Sometimes they join in a communal *Seder* or gather with in-laws or relatives and friends who attended other first night *Sedarim*. The second *Seder* may follow the same pattern as the first or may have another focus, such as the liberation of specific oppressed Jewish communities. A second *Seder* may provide the opportunity to add passages omitted on the first night.

B-5   The *mitzvah* of hospitality (*Hachnasat Orechim*)

הַכְנָסַת
אוֹרְחִים
It is a *mitzvah* to invite guests to join in the *Seder*. So important is it that the invitation is included in the text of the *Haggadah*, "Let all who are hungry come and eat, let all who are in want share the hope of Passover."[148] Arrangements should be made to see that no one has to celebrate Passover alone. Many communities make special arrangements for those who are alone, including the elderly, widows, widowers, and college students who are away from home.

B-6   The *mitzvah* of *Tzedakah*

צְדָקָה
מְעוֹת חִטִּין
It is a *mitzvah* to give *Tzedakah* before the beginning of Passover.[149] Tradition encourages the solicitation of special funds (*Me-ot Chitin*) to provide a proper *Seder* for the poor.[150]

*The Central Conference of American Rabbis has published *A Passover Haggadah*, edited by Rabbi Herbert Bronstein and illustrated by Leonard Baskin, with essays by Lawrence A. Hoffman and W. Gunther Plaut.

B-7 The *mitzvah* of participating in the *Seder* and reciting the *Haggadah*

הַגָּדָה

It is a *mitzvah* for every Jew to participate in the recitation of the *Haggadah*, which recalls the Exodus from Egypt.[151] All should look upon themselves as having personally experienced the Exodus. "In every generation, each person should feel as though he/she personally had gone forth from Egypt, as it is written: 'And you shall explain to your child on that day, it is because of what the Lord did for me when I *myself* went forth from Egypt.' "[152]

B-8 The *Seder* Plate

מַצָּה
לֶחֶם מִשְׁנֶה

זְרוֹעַ
כַּרְפַּס

מָרוֹר

חֲרֹסֶת
בֵּיצָה
חֲגִיגָה

In front of the leader or in front of each participant, a special *Seder* Plate is set.[153] The following are arranged on it: three separate pieces of *Matzah*—two pieces represent the two traditional loaves (*Lechem Mishneh*) set out in the ancient Temple during Sabbaths and Festivals, and the third *Matzah* is symbolic of Passover; a roasted shankbone (*Zeroa*) burned or scorched, representing the ancient Passover sacrifice; parsley or green herbs (*Karpas*), symbolizing the growth of springtime, the green of hope and renewal; the top part of horseradish root (*Maror*), symbolic of the bitterness that our ancestors experienced in Egypt and, in a contemporary sense, the lot of all who are enslaved; *Charoset*, representing the mortar which our ancestors used for Pharaoh's labor; a roasted egg (*Beitsah*), representing the *Chagigah* or festival offering, a symbol of life itself, the triumph of life over death.

B-9 The Cup of Elijah

A special cup filled with wine is placed prominently on the table. In popular legend the Prophet Elijah (herald of redemption) visits every Jewish home at some time during the *Seder*. Therefore, one cup of wine is set aside for him.[154] After the meal, one of the participants, usually a young child, opens the door for Elijah. This is a moment filled with hope and anticipation.

B-10 The *mitzvah* of eating unleavened bread (*Matzah*)

מַצָּה   It is a *mitzvah* to eat *Matzah* during the *Seder* and to recite the appropriate blessings.[155]

בָּרוּךְ אַתָּה, יְיָ אֱלֹהֵינוּ, מֶלֶךְ הָעוֹלָם, הַמּוֹצִיא לֶחֶם מִן הָאָרֶץ.

Ba-ruch a-ta, A-do-nai E-lo-hei-nu, me-lech ha-o-lam, ha-mo-tsi le-chem min ha-a-rets.

Blessed is the Lord our God, Ruler of the universe, Who brings forth bread from the earth.

בָּרוּךְ אַתָּה, יְיָ אֱלֹהֵינוּ, מֶלֶךְ הָעוֹלָם, אֲשֶׁר קִדְּשָׁנוּ בְּמִצְוֹתָיו וְצִוָּנוּ
עַל אֲכִילַת מַצָּה.

Ba-ruch a-ta, A-do-nai E-lo-hei-nu, me-lech ha-o-lam, a-sher ki-de-sha-nu be-mits-vo-tav ve-tsi-va-nu al a-chi-lat ma-tsa.

Blessed is the Lord our God, Ruler of the universe, Who hallows our lives with commandments, Who has commanded us regarding the eating of Matzah.

By eating *Matzah* we recall that the dough prepared by our people had no time to rise before the final act of redemption. "And they baked unleavened cakes of the dough since they had been driven out of Egypt and could not delay, nor had they prepared provisions for them-selves."[156]

B-11 The *mitzvah* of eating bitter herbs (*Maror*)

It is a *mitzvah* to eat *Maror*, the bitter herbs, with the appropriate blessing.[157]

בָּרוּךְ אַתָּה, יְיָ אֱלֹהֵינוּ, מֶלֶךְ הָעוֹלָם,
אֲשֶׁר קִדְּשָׁנוּ בְּמִצְוֹתָיו וְצִוָּנוּ עַל אֲכִילַת מָרוֹר.

Ba-ruch a-ta, A-do-nai E-lo-hei-nu, me-lech ha-o-lam, a-sher ki-de-sha-nu be-mits-vo-tav ve-tsi-va-nu al a-chi-lat ma-ror.

Blessed is the Lord our God, Ruler of the universe, Who hallows our lives through commandments, Who has commanded us regarding the eating of Maror.

Maror is eaten because the Egyptians embittered the lives of our people, as it is written: "With hard labor at mortar and brick and in all sorts of work in the field, with all the tasks ruthlessly imposed upon them."[158]

B-12 The *Matzah* of Hope

Many families in our generation set aside an extra *Matzah*, called the Matzah of Hope, for the Jews of the Soviet Union whose lives are bitter as were the lives of our enslaved ancestors. Another way to dramatize the endangered existence of Soviet Jews is to place an empty chair at the *Seder* table to remind us of them.

B-13 The *mitzvah* of Four Cups

It is a *mitzvah* to drink four cups of wine during the *Seder*.[159] Some follow the custom of adding a fifth cup.[160]

B-14 The Four Questions

It is customary for the youngest participant or participants to recite the Four Questions.[161] These questions point to the unusual features of the *Seder* meal and provide an opportunity to teach the lesson of Passover. The text may be found in *A Passover Haggadah*, page 29.

B-15 Reclining

It is the custom to simulate a reclining position while eating by propping oneself up with cushions.[162] Reclining at the *Seder* is symbolic of being free people who are able to eat with leisure.

B-16 Afikoman

אֲפִיקוֹמָן   The *Afikoman* is the half *Matzah* that is set aside during the breaking of the *Matzah* early in the *Seder*. An old tradition held that the group could not leave the *Seder* table unless all had tasted of the *Afikoman*.[163] In connection with this, and in order to arouse and maintain the interest of the children and to provide some entertainment for them, a practice developed of *hiding* and searching for the *Afikoman*. Sometime during the meal, the leader hides the *Afikoman* trying to elude the watchful observance of the children, whose endeavor it is to search out its hiding place. Prizes might be awarded to all who participated, with a special gift to the one who actually finds it. In some households it is the custom for children to "steal" the *Afikoman* in order to hide it and hold it for "ransom," since the meal cannot conclude without it.

B-17 Chol Hamo-ed

חוֹל הַמּוֹעֵד   The intermediate days, between the first and the seventh days, are known as *Chol Hamo-ed*. During this period no leaven is eaten.[164] Every effort is made to preserve the holiday mood.

B-18 The Song of Songs

שִׁיר   On the Shabbat during Pesach, the Song of Songs (*Shir*
הַשִּׁירִים   *Hashirim*) is read.[165] The Song of Songs refers to spring-

time, and thus befits the festival. In addition, Jewish tradition has interpreted Song of Songs as an allegory of the love of God for Israel. The experiences of hope and redemption, which characterize Pesach, make the Song of Songs particularly appropriate to this season.

B-19 The *mitzvah* of *Yizkor*

יִזְכֹּר   It is a *mitzvah* to recite *Yizkor* on the seventh day of Pesach.[166] It memorializes our relatives and our own friends, as well as the martyrs of our generation and previous generations (see *Gates of Mitzvah*, page 63, D-10, and "*Yizkor*," pages 153–155).

B-20 The study of *Pirkei Avot*

פִּרְקֵי אָבוֹת   Beginning with the first Shabbat after Pesach, it is customary to study one of the chapters of *Pirkei Avot* (*Ethics of the Fathers*) each Shabbat afternoon until Shavuot. Selections from *Pirkei Avot* can be found in *Gates of Prayer*, pages 16–28. *Pirkei Avot* is devoted to the ethical-religious maxims of the Rabbis. The study of this material is part of the preparation for Shavuot. As we complete each weekly study session, we are one week closer to Shavuot and מַתַּן תּוֹרָה the recollection of *Matan Torah*, the giving of commandments at Sinai.

SHAVUOT

You shall observe the Feast of Weeks, of the first
fruits of the wheat harvest.

—EXODUS 34:22

On the day of the first fruits, your Feast of
Weeks, when you bring an offering of new grain
to the Lord, you shall observe a holy day.

—NUMBERS 28:26

You shall count off seven weeks; start to count
the seven weeks when the sickle is first put to the
standing grain. Then you shall observe the Feast
of Weeks for the Lord your God, offering a free
will contribution according as the Lord your God
has blessed you.

—DEUTERONOMY 16:9–10

SHAVUOT occurs on the sixth of the Hebrew month of Sivan. The name *Shavuot* ("weeks") derives from its celebration seven weeks (a week of weeks) after Pesach.[167] In the Torah it is also designated by the names *Chag Hakatsir*, the Harvest Festival (Exodus 23:16), and *Chag Habikurim*, the Festival of First Fruits (Exodus 34:22).

Current observance is based on the Talmudic identification of Shavuot with the events at Sinai.[168] Therefore it is called *Zeman matan toratenu,*" the season of the giving of the Torah. On Shavuot, the Jewish people celebrate their covenantal relationship with God and reaffirm their commitment to a Jewish life of study (*Talmud Torah*) and practice (*mitzvah*). The significance of the events at Sinai derives not only from the receiving of *mitzvot* but also from their acceptance, as is illustrated in Israel's response, "*Na-aseh venishma,*" "We will faithfully do."[169] Sinai represents a constant effort to confront life and history in light of this covenantal relationship.

The ceremony of Confirmation is a Reform innovation and has added a new dimension to the meaning of the Festival. It provides an opportunity for students of post-Bar/Bat Mitzvah age to affirm their relationship to Judaism and the Jewish people.

C.   SHAVUOT

C-1   The *mitzvah* of observing Shavuot

שָׁבוּעוֹת   It is a *mitzvah* to observe Shavuot seven weeks after Passover, on the 6th of Sivan. As it is said, "From the day which you bring the sheaf of wave offering, the day after the Sabbath [understood by the Rabbis to mean the first day of Passover],[170] you will count seven weeks. They must be completed, and you must count until the day after the seventh week—fifty days. . . . On that same day you shall hold a celebration. It will be a holy day for you" (Leviticus 23:15–16, 21).

C-2 Decorating the home and synagogue

בִּכּוּרִים

It is customary to decorate one's home and the synagogue with greens and fresh flowers on Shavuot.[171] The greenery is a reminder of the ancient practice of bringing first fruits (*Bikurim*) to the Temple in Jerusalem. It also calls to mind our hopes for an abundant harvest.

C-3 The *mitzvah* of reaffirming the covenant

תַּלְמוּד תּוֹרָה

עַם בְּרִית

תִּקּוּן לֵיל שָׁבוּעוֹת

It is a *mitzvah* to reaffirm the covenant on Shavuot.[172] Through the reading of the Ten Commandments at services, which recalls the establishment of the covenant and the contemplation of the importance of Torah and its lifelong study (*Talmud Torah*), the individual Jew and the community renew their commitment to be a Covenant People (*Am Berit*).

As part of the celebration of Shavuot a number of congregations have revived the old custom of studying Torah late into Shavuot night.[173] This Torah vigil is called *Tikun Leil Shavuot*.

C-4 Attending Confirmation Service

The ceremony of Confirmation is one of the highlights of Shavuot observance.[174] When the Temple stood, Jews brought offerings of first fruits, *Bikurim*, to the Temple on Shavuot. Today, parents bring their children to participate in Confirmation. These young people are the first fruits of each year's harvest. They represent the hope and promise of tomorrow. During the service the confirmands reaffirm their commitment to the covenant. "[The Confirmation's] purpose is to encourage the intellectual and spiritual growth of young people, and to strengthen the

bonds between them and the Israelites who received the
Torah at Sinai (Exodus 19:3–8 and Deuteronomy 29:9–14),
and to stimulate their love for God and the Jewish people"
(*Gates of Mitzvah*, page 22, E-8).

C-5   Reading of the Book of Ruth

מְגִלַּת רוּת   The Book of Ruth (*Megilat Rut*) is read on Shavuot.[175]
The story of Ruth takes place during the barley harvest
at the Shavuot season. More important, Rabbinic tradition
has seen a parallel between Ruth's willing acceptance of
Judaism and the Jewish people's acceptance of Torah.[176]

C-6   Special foods

It is customary to eat dairy dishes on Shavuot. Rabbinic
tradition draws an analogy between the sweetness and
physical nourishment the Jew receives from milk and honey to the sweetness and spiritual nourishment of the words
of Torah.[177]

C-7   *Yizkor* on Shavuot

יִזְכֹּר   While it is the practice of the majority of Reform congregations to recite *Yizkor* only on Yom Kippur and the
seventh day of Pesach, some congregations follow the tradition of having *Yizkor* services on Shavuot.[178] In such
cases, it is a *mitzvah* to join with the congregation in
reciting *Yizkor*. It memorializes our deceased friends and
relatives as well as the martyrs of our generation and
previous generations (see *Gates of Mitzvah*, page 63, D-
10, and "*Yizkor*," pages 153–155).

SUKKOT (INCLUDING ATSERET/ SIMCHAT TORAH)

On the fifteenth day of this seventh month there shall be the Feast of Booths to the Lord seven days.

—LEVITICUS 23:34

After the ingathering from your threshing floor and your vat, you shall hold the Feast of Booths for seven days.

—DEUTERONOMY 16:13

On the eighth day you shall observe a sacred occasion.

—LEVITICUS 23:36

SUKKOT begins on the fifteenth of the Hebrew month of Tishri, and concludes on the twenty-second with Atseret/Simchat Torah. Sukkot is the fall harvest festival.[179] The eighth day, Atseret, functions as the conclusion of Sukkot but is also a separate festival.[180] Since Reform Jews follow the calendar of the Torah and (like the Jew living in Israel) do not add a ninth day to the Festival, they celebrate Simchat Torah and Atseret on the same day.

More than any other of the Pilgrimage Festivals, Sukkot has retained its agricultural character. However, Sukkot is also the commemoration of a significant event in the life of the Jewish people: the journey through the wilderness toward the Land of Israel. The Torah identifies the *Sukkah* (booth) with the temporary dwellings in which the Israelites lived during that journey (Levicitus 23:42).

The mood of Sukkot is particularly joyous. Its beautiful symbolism of the successful harvest provides a welcome change of religious pace from the solemn days of prayer and introspection of Rosh Hashanah and Yom Kippur. While all of the Three Pilgrimage Festivals are times of rejoicing, Sukkot is specifically designated as *"Zeman simchatenu,"* the season of our rejoicing.[181] Even while we rejoice, the *Sukkah's* temporary and fragile structure reminds us how precarious life may be.

Through the use of the *Lulav* and *Etrog*[182] we acknowledge our dependence upon God for the food we eat. Living in an urban environment, it is easy to forget that both human labor and divine blessing make the world fruitful. On Sukkot our thoughts turn to the wonder and beauty of the world, to our responsibilities as its caretakers, and to our obligation to share, for God is the true owner of the land and its produce.

Atseret/Simchat Torah is the day on which we finish reading the last verses of Deuteronomy and immediately begin again with the first verses of Genesis. The Torah scrolls are removed from the Ark and carried around the synagogue. The celebration is one of unbridled joy as we express our happiness at having lived to complete the reading of the Torah yet another time and to begin reading it again.

D. SUKKOT (INCLUDING ATSERET/ SIMCHAT TORAH)

D-1 The *mitzvah* of observing Sukkot

It is a *mitzvah* to observe Sukkot from the fifteenth of the Hebrew month of Tishri for seven days and to conclude on the twenty-second (the eighth day) with the observance of Atseret/Simchat Torah. As the Torah says, "On the fifteenth day of the seventh month there shall be a Feast of Booths to the Lord seven days. . . . On the eighth day you shall observe a holy day" (Leviticus 23:34, 36).

D-2 The *mitzvah* of rejoicing

It is a *mitzvah* to rejoice on Sukkot. As the Torah teaches, "You shall rejoice on your festival . . . for the Lord your God will bless all your crops and all your undertakings, and you shall have nothing but joy" (Deuteronomy 16:14, 15). While rejoicing is a *mitzvah* on all of the Three Pilgrimage Festivals, it is characteristic of the observance of Sukkot. So much so that the tradition has designated

זְמַן שִׂמְחָתֵנוּ   it as "*Zeman simchatenu*," the season of our rejoicing.

D-3 The *mitzvah* of *Tzedakah*

צְדָקָה   It is always a *mitzvah* to give *Tzedakah*.[183] However, since on Sukkot we give thanks for the harvest, all the more should we feel obliged to share with those who are less fortunate than we.

D-4   The *mitzvah* of building a *Sukkah*

סֻכָּה   It is a *mitzvah* for every Jew to participate in the building and decoration of a *Sukkah*.[184] It is particularly meritorious to begin the construction of the *Sukkah* immediately after the conclusion of Yom Kippur services (see "Yom Kippur," C-13, page 54). The *Sukkah* may be built in a yard or on a roof or balcony. Since many Jewish people live in apartments and in other locations where the construction of a *Sukkah* is not feasible, it is suggested that one aid in the building or decorating of the *Sukkah* at the synagogue, the community center, or the home of friends.

D-5   The *mitzvah* of *Lulav* and *Etrog*

לוּלָב   It is a *mitzvah* to take up the *Lulav* and *Etrog* and recite
אֶתְרוֹג   the appropriate blessing at any time during the whole day of Sukkot.[185]

בָּרוּךְ אַתָּה, יְיָ אֱלֹהֵינוּ, מֶלֶךְ הָעוֹלָם, אֲשֶׁר קִדְּשָׁנוּ בְּמִצְוֹתָיו
וְצִוָּנוּ עַל נְטִילַת לוּלָב.

Ba-ruch a-ta, A-do-nai E-lo-hei-nu, me-lech ha-o-lam, a-sher ki-de-sha-nu be-mits-vo-tav ve-tsi-va-nu al ne-ti-lat lu-lav.

Blessed is the Lord our God, Ruler of the universe, by Whose mitzvot we are hallowed, Who gives us the mitzvah of Lulav.

The text of the blessing and additional prayers may be found in *Gates of the House*, page 78, and *Gates of Prayer*, page 524. By taking up the *Lulav* and *Etrog* and waving them in all directions, one symbolically acknowledges the sovereignty of God over all nature.[186]

אַרְבָּעָה   The *Lulav* and *Etrog* are also called the four species
מִינִים   (*Arba-ah Minim*). They consist of *Etrog* (citron), *Lulav*
אֶתְרוֹג, לוּלָב   (palm), *Hadas* (myrtle), and *Aravah* (willow). The iden-
הֲדַס, עֲרָבָה   tification of the four species is based on the Rabbinic

interpretation of Leviticus 23:40, "On the first day you shall take the product of the *Hadar* trees, branches of palm trees, boughs of leafy trees, and willows of the brook."[187]

הָדָר

The *Etrog* has maintained a separate identity. Two willow branches and three myrtle branches are bound together around one palm branch and are called the *Lulav*.[188]

It is desirable to acquire a *Lulav* and *Etrog*, and it is preferable, where possible, to select one's own set.[189] By selecting a beautiful *Lulav* and *Etrog* one enhances the performance of the *mitzvah* (see "*Hidur Mitzvah*: The Aesthetics of *Mitzvot*," pages 162–164).

D-6 The *mitzvah* of celebrating in the *Sukkah*

It is a *mitzvah* to celebrate in the *Sukkah*. The Torah says, "You shall live in booths seven days in order that the future generations may know that I made the Israelite people live in booths when I brought them out of the land of Egypt" (Leviticus 23:42–43).

The Torah speaks of living in the *Sukkah* for seven days. Where climate and circumstances permit, some will want to do so. However, others will prefer to fulfill this *mitzvah* by eating in the *Sukkah* (either a whole meal or a symbolic meal or by making *Kiddush* there). When eating or reciting *Kiddush* in the *Sukkah*, a special blessing is recited:

בָּרוּךְ אַתָּה, יְיָ אֱלֹהֵינוּ, מֶלֶךְ הָעוֹלָם, אֲשֶׁר קִדְּשָׁנוּ בְּמִצְוֹתָיו
וְצִוָּנוּ לֵישֵׁב בַּסֻּכָּה.

Ba-ruch a-ta, A-do-nai E-lo-hei-nu, me-lech ha-o-lam, a-sher ki-de-sha-nu be-mi-ts-vo-tav ve-tsi-va-nu lei-shev ba-su-ka.

Blessed is the Lord our God, Ruler of the Universe, Who hallows us with His mitzvot and commands us to celebrate in the Sukkah.

When circumstances do not permit one to fulfill this *mitzvah* in one's own *Sukkah*, one should seek out the *Sukkah* at the synagogue, at the community center, or at the home of friends.

D-7   The *mitzvah* of hospitality (*Hachnasat Orechim*)

הַכְנָסַת
אוֹרְחִים
אֻשְׁפִּיזִין

As part of the *mitzvah* of hospitality we are urged to share our meals in gratitude for God's gifts.[190] There is a ceremony of welcoming guests known as *Ushpizin*, which evokes the presence of the patriarchs and matriarchs as our spiritual companions in the *Sukkah*. (The text may be found in *Gates of the House*, pages 77–78.)

D-8   Reading of Kohelet

קֹהֶלֶת

The Book of Kohelet (Ecclesiastes) is read on the Shabbat during Sukkot.[191] Like the *Sukkah*, it reminds us of the transitory nature of life.

D-9   *Chol Hamo-ed*

חוֹל הַמּוֹעֵד

The intermediate days of Sukkot are known as *Chol Hamo-ed*. The *mitzvot* of celebrating in the *Sukkah* and blessing the *Lulav* can be performed. Each day can be an opportunity for rejoicing and for preserving the festival atmosphere.[192]

D-10 Atseret/Simchat Torah

Atseret/Simchat Torah follows the seventh day of Sukkot[193] and is celebrated as a day of rejoicing. The *mitzvot* which are common to all the other Festivals are observed on Atseret/Simchat Torah (see "The Pilgrimage Festivals," A-3, page 61).

D-11 The *mitzvah* of completing and beginning the Torah cycle on Atseret/Simchat Torah

It is a *mitzvah* to participate in the Torah procession honoring the completion and beginning of the Torah-reading

cycle and to hear the reading of the end of Deuteronomy
and the beginning of Genesis.[194] Jewish tradition has divided the Torah into weekly portions so that one reads
through the entire Torah each year. The completion of the
reading of the Torah is a time of rejoicing and an opportunity to express love for Torah. Immediately after com-
pleting the reading of the last verses of Deuteronomy, the
first verses of Genesis are read to indicate that the study
of Torah never ends. It symbolizes our obligation to ob-
תַּלְמוּד תּוֹרָה   serve the *mitzvah* of *Talmud Torah* constantly.

D-12 The *mitzvah* of *Yizkor*

יִזְכּוֹר   While it is the practice of the majority of Reform congregations to recite *Yizkor* only on Yom Kippur and the
seventh day of Pesach, some congregations follow the tradition of having *Yizkor* services on Atseret/Simchat Torah.[195] In such cases, it is a *mitzvah* to join with the
congregation in reciting *Yizkor*. It memorializes our deceased friends and relatives as well as the martyrs of our
generation and previous generations (see *Gates of Mitzvah*,
page 63, D-10, and "*Yizkor*," pages 153–155).

D-13 Consecration

Since Simchat Torah is a joyful affirmation of the *mitzvah*
of Torah Study, some congregations hold a special ceremony for children entering religious school for the first
time. The ceremony, called Consecration, emphasizes the
importance and joy of *Talmud Torah* in Jewish tradition.
It is also the custom at Consecration to give the children
something sweet so that they may look upon the learning
of Torah as sweet.[196] In addition, many congregations present the children with miniature Torah scrolls, which the
children then keep in a special place.

חֲנֻכָּה
פּוּרִים

Chanukah
Purim

CHANUKAH

Now on the 25th day of the ninth month, which
is called the month of Kislev, in the 148th year,
they rose up in the morning and offered sacrifice
according to the law upon the new altar of burnt
offerings, which they had made. At the very
season and on the very day that the Gentiles had
profaned it, it was dedicated with songs, citherns,
harps, and cymbals. . . . And so they kept the
dedication of the altar eight days. . . . Moreover,
Judah and his brethren, with the whole
congregation of Israel, ordained that the days of
the dedication of the altar should be kept in their
season from year to year for eight days, from the
25th day of the month Kislev, with mirth and
gladness.

—I MACCABEES 4:52–59

What is Chanukah? For the rabbis have taught:
Commencing with the 25th day of the month of
Kislev, there are eight days upon which there
shall be neither mourning nor fasting. For when
the Hellenists entered the Temple, they defiled all
the oil that was there. It was when the might of
the Hasmonean dynasty overcame and
vanquished them that, upon search, only a single
cruse of undefiled oil, sealed by the High Priest,
was found. In it was oil enough for the needs of
a single day. A miracle was wrought and it
burned eight days. The next year they ordained
these days a holiday with songs and praises.

—TALMUD B., SHABBAT 21b

CHANUKAH begins on the 25th day of the Hebrew month of Kislev and lasts for eight days. It commemorates the victory of Judah Maccabee and his followers over the forces of the Syrian tyrant Antiochus Ephiphanes and the rededication of the Temple in Jerusalem which the Syrians had profaned. Chanukah celebrates more than the end of an unsuccessful attempt by an outside power to destroy Judaism. The threat to Judaism was both internal and external. The assimilation to Hellenistic culture was so great that certain elements within Jewish society sought to become fully assimilated, to be accepted as Greek citizens and to participate in Greek culture at the expense of their own unique Judaic culture. The resistance of the Maccabees and their allies to the blandishments of assimilation preserved Judaism. The story of Chanukah is the age-old struggle of the Jewish people to remain Jewish in a non-Jewish world.

To celebrate their victory and to rededicate the Temple, the Maccabees proclaimed an eight-day festival, which was to be observed annually.[197] According to the Talmudic legend, when the Hasmoneans recaptured and cleansed the Temple, they were able to find only a single cruse of oil with the seal of the High Priest, sufficient for one day's lighting of the *Menorah*. But, as the story goes, a miracle occurred, and it burned for eight days.[198]

The nightly kindling of the *Menorah* with its increasingly brighter light has become a symbol for both our physical and spiritual resistance to tyranny and assimilation.[199] Jewish tradition has preserved this twofold concept of resistance. The heroic Maccabean triumph is counter-balanced by the words of the prophet Zechariah: "Not by might and not by power, but by My Spirit, says the Lord (4:6)."[200]

A.   CHANUKAH

A-1   The *mitzvah* of observing Chanukah

It is a *mitzvah* to observe Chanukah for eight days. The
Rabbis taught: "Commencing with the twenty-fifth of Kislev, there are eight days upon which there shall be neither
mourning nor fasting."[201]

A-2   The *mitzvah* of kindling Chanukah lights

It is a *mitzvah* to kindle the Chanukah lights in one's
home with the appropriate blessing:[202]

בָּרוּךְ אַתָּה, יְיָ אֱלֹהֵינוּ, מֶלֶךְ הָעוֹלָם, אֲשֶׁר קִדְּשָׁנוּ בְּמִצְוֹתָיו וְצִוְּנוּ
לְהַדְלִיק נֵר שֶׁל חֲנֻכָּה.

Ba-ruch a-ta, A-do-nai E-lo-hei-nu, me-lech, ha-o-
lam, a-sher ki-de-sha-nu be-mits-vo-tav ve-tsi-va-nu
le-had-lik ner shel Cha-nu-ka.

Blessed is the Lord our God, Ruler of the Universe, by Whose
mitzvot we are hallowed, Who commands us to kindle the
Chanuka lights.

בָּרוּךְ אַתָּה, יְיָ אֱלֹהֵינוּ, מֶלֶךְ הָעוֹלָם, שֶׁעָשָׂה נִסִּים לַאֲבוֹתֵינוּ
בַּיָּמִים הָהֵם, בַּזְּמַן הַזֶּה.

Ba-ruch a-ta, A-do-nai E-lo-hei-nu, me-lech ha-o-
lam, she-a-sa ni-sim la-a-vo-tei-nu ba-ya-mim ha-
hem ba-ze-man ha-zeh.

Blessed is the Lord our God, Ruler of the Universe, Who
performed wondrous deeds for our ancestors in days of old, at
this season.

ON FIRST NIGHT ONLY:

בָּרוּךְ אַתָּה, יְיָ אֱלֹהֵינוּ, מֶלֶךְ הָעוֹלָם, שֶׁהֶחֱיָנוּ וְקִיְּמָנוּ וְהִגִּיעָנוּ לַזְּמַן הַזֶּה.

Ba-ruch a-ta, A-do-nai, E-lo-hei-nu, me-lech ha-o-lam, she-he-che-ya-nu ve-ki-ye-ma-nu ve-hi-gi-a-nu la-ze-man ha-zeh.

Blessed is the Lord our God, Ruler of the Universe, for giving us life, for sustaining us, and for enabling us to reach this season.

Appropriate readings for each night may be found in *Gates of the House*, pages 80–85.

One candle is lit for each night. The candle for the first night is placed on the right side of the special eight-branched *Menorah* (or *Chanukiyah*). On each subsequent night, an additional candle is placed to the left of the preceding night's candle. The lighting proceeds from left to right so that the new candle is kindled first. No practical use may be made of the Chanukah lights, such as illuminating the room. Therefore, according to Jewish tradition, a special candle known as the *Shamash* is used to light the others and to provide light.[203]

מְנוֹרָה
חֲנֻכִּיָּה

שַׁמָּשׁ

On Friday night the Chanukah lights are lit before Shabbat candles, and on Saturday night at *Havdalah*.[204] The kindling of Chanukah lights in the synagogue is no substitute for kindling them at home.

A-3   Displaying the *Chanukiyah*

חֲנֻכִּיָּה It is an old custom to place the *Chanukiyah* where its lights will be visible from the outside.[205] The public proclamation of the miracle of Chanukah is part of the observance of the holiday. Displaying the *Chanukiyah* is a demonstration of the Jew's pride and identity.

A-4 Special foods

It is the custom to eat dairy dishes during Chanukah, as well as food cooked in oil.[206] Among Ashkenazi Jews, the most frequently served dish is potato *Latkes*. However, some have adopted the oriental Jewish custom prevalent in Israel of serving *Sufganiyot* (jelly doughnuts). The serving of special foods adds to the enjoyment of the holiday (see "Festival Foods," pages 159–162).

A-5 *Dreidel*

The playing of games has long been associated with Chanukah. The most popular is the game of *Dreidel* (or *Sevivon*.)[207] *Dreidel* is a four-sided top with the Hebrew letters *Nun, Gimel, He,* and *Shin* inscribed on its sides. The letters have been popularly identified as mnemonic for *Nes Gadol Haya Sham*, "A great miracle happened there."[208]

A-6 Chanukah gifts

Many people exchange gifts during Chanukah and/or give small sums of money to children. These practices are part of Chanukah's special appeal to children during what has become (in our society) a time of almost universal gift giving. While this practice can add to the enjoyment of the holiday, undue emphasis should not be placed upon the giving and receiving of gifts. When money is given, children should be encouraged to use some of it for *Tzedakah*. In any case, it is important to stress the real message of Chanukah, the struggle of the Jewish people to remain distinctive in a non-Jewish world.

PURIM

The rest of the Jews, those in the king's
provinces, likewise mustered and fought for their
lives. . . . That was on the thirteenth day of the
month of Adar; and they rested on the
fourteenth day and made it a day of feasting and
merrymaking. (But the Jews in Shushan
mustered on both the thirteenth and fourteenth
days, and so rested on the fifteenth and made it
a day of feasting and merrymaking.) That is why
village Jews, who live in unwalled towns, observe
the fourteenth day of the month of Adar and
make it a day of merrymaking and feasting, and
as a holiday and an occasion for sending gifts to
one another.

—Esther 9:16–19

PURIM, which occurs on the fourteenth of the Hebrew month of Adar (the fifteenth in Jerusalem),[209] is a celebration of the events described in the Scroll of Esther (*Megilat Ester*). The holiday with its joyous carnival-like atmosphere focuses on one of the main themes in Jewish history, i.e., the survival of the Jewish people despite the attempts of their enemies to destroy them. According to the Scroll of Esther, the name Purim is derived from the lot (*Pur*) cast by Haman to determine the day on which the Jews would be exterminated (Esther 3:7).

The story of Purim is about hunger for power and about hatred born of the Jews' refusal to assimilate and their unwillingness to compromise religious principle by bowing before the secular authority. It is an old story. However, it has been repeated many times, making it both an ancient and modern story.[210]

In the story it is related that Mordecai, Esther's cousin, refused to prostrate himself before Haman, the vizier of King Ahasuerus. So infuriated was Haman that he sought the annihilation of the Jewish people. Haman's accusation against the Jewish people has become the paradigm for all anti-Semites: "There is a certain people scattered abroad and dispersed among the peoples . . . their laws are different from those of other people, they do not obey the king's law, and the king should not tolerate them" (Esther 3:8). The prudent actions of Mordecai and the courage of Esther averted tragedy.

Purim recalls the dangers of minority status. Hatred of the foreigner and the stranger is still prevalent throughout the world. Anti-Semitism has not disappeared, but despite everything, the Jewish people has survived. Purim, however, is most of all a happy story—a story of survival and triumph over evil.

B.   PURIM

B-1   The *mitzvah* of observing Purim

It is a *mitzvah* to observe Purim on the fourteenth of
Adar.[211] This is based on the statement, "The Jews of the
villages that lived in unwalled towns made the 14th of
the month of Adar a day of gladness and feasting, a holiday, and of sending gifts to one another" (*Esther* 9:19).

B-2   The *mitzvah* of reading the Scroll of Esther (*Megilat Ester*)

מְגִלַּת אֶסְתֵּר   It is a *mitzvah* to read the Biblical Scroll of Esther (*Megilat
Ester*) and to celebrate the holiday with the congrega-
tion.[212] If illness or emergency prevents attendance at services, one may fulfill the *mitzvah* by reading the Book of
Esther at home.

As part of the *Megilah* reading, it is customary for the
listeners to attempt to drown out the sound of Haman's
name by shouting or using *Greggers* (*Ra-ashanim*—special
noise makers).[213]

B-3   Rejoicing and feasting

The almost unrestrained merriment which pervades the
celebration of Purim makes it unique among the Jewish
holidays.[214] Adults and children are encouraged to wear
costumes.[215] Synagogues and communities stage Purim
plays, hold carnivals, and serve festive communal meals.
All these activities are an expression of great joy at having
survived Haman and countless other enemies.

B-4   Special foods

In Ashkenazi communities, *Hamantaschen*, three-cornered
cookies filled with poppy seeds or other fruits, are served
on Purim. In many Sephardic communities and in Israel,
אָזְנֵי הָמָן   pastries called Haman's ears, *Oznei Haman*, are served (see
"Festival Foods," pages 159–162).

B-5   The sending of portions (*Mishloach Manot*)

מִשְׁלוֹחַ מָנוֹת   Traditionally Purim is a time for exchanging gifts. It is customary to send gifts of food or pastries to friends and family. The sending of these gifts is called *Mishloach Manot*, "the sending of portions."[216] (In popular pronunciation this custom is called *Shalach Mones.*)

B-6   The *mitzvah* of sending gifts to the poor

It is a *mitzvah* to send gifts to the poor on Purim.[217] The sending of gifts to the poor is an act of *Tzedakah* which is especially connected with Purim.

Other Special Days

A.   ROSH CHODESH (NEW MONTH)

THE months of the Hebrew calendar are determined by the re-
curring phases of the moon: the new month begins when the
new moon appears.* From the earliest times, the lunar month was
far more than a measuring device for Jews. The cycles of *Hama-or
Hakatan*, "the lesser light" (Genesis 1:16), served as a reminder of
God's work of creation, and led naturally to the celebration of the
new moon as an important festival in Biblical times.[218] The major
festivals, with the exception of Shabbat, in turn, were dated by the
new moon's occurrence.

The Mishnah describes in detail the procedure by which the new
month was fixed in the days before the destruction of the Temple.[219]
That catastrophe, combined with the development of a scientifically
calculated calendar in the Talmudic period, served to diminish the
significance of Rosh Chodesh, reducing it to a minor festival. Its
observance today is generally limited to its proclamation in certain
synagogues on the preceding Shabbat and to some liturgical changes
in the service on the day of Rosh Chodesh.[220]

The one unusual feature of Rosh Chodesh is that, while it remained
an ordinary workday for men, an ancient tradition declares it a wom-
en's holiday. Jewish women were to refrain from all work, or at least
heavy work, on that day.[221] According to legend, God rewarded them
with a special day of rest for refusing to join with the Israelite men
in the sin of the Golden Calf.[222] Today, many Jewish women are
reviving and reinterpreting this Rosh Chodesh tradition.[223] But Rosh
Chodesh stands as a reminder to all Jews—women and men—of a
special and distinct rhythm in our lives—the rhythm of Jewish time.

*See "The Jewish Calendar," pages 7–11.

B.   *YOM HA-ATSMA-UT*
(ISRAEL INDEPENDENCE DAY)

ON the fifth day of the Hebrew month of Iyar 5708 (May 14, 1948), Israel was reborn as a modern, independent state. Since that time Jews throughout the world have celebrated the day in commemoration and rejoicing. In response to the widespread observance of Yom Ha-Atsma-ut among Reform Jews, the Central Conference of American Rabbis, at its convention on Mount Scopus in 1970, proclaimed Israel Independence Day "a permanent annual festival in the religious calendar of Reform Judaism."[224] In addition, the Reform Movement has published a special worship service to mark the occasion and has provided special Torah and *Haftarah* readings for the day (see *Gates of Prayer*, pages 590–611, and *Gates of the House*, page 295).

The celebration of Yom Ha-Atsma-ut recognizes that a new era has dawned in the life of the Jewish people. It attests to the essential unity of the whole household of Israel, and marks the cultural and spiritual renaissance which draws strength from the symbiotic relationship between Israel and world Jewry. The rebirth of Israel from the ashes of the *Sho-ah* is a symbol of hope against despair, of redemption against devastation.

It is a *mitzvah* for every Jew to mark Yom Ha-Atsma-ut by participation in public worship services and/or celebrations which affirm the bond between the Jews living in the Land of Israel and those living outside. Furthermore, a special act of *Tzedakah* to an organization or institution which helps to strengthen the State of Israel would be a significant way of affirming the unity of the Jewish people. One may wish to have a festive meal on Yom Ha-Atsma-ut at which one serves foods from Israel and sings Israeli songs.

C.   *YOM HASHO-AH (HOLOCAUST DAY)*

THE twenty-seventh of the Hebrew month of Nisan, called Yom HaSho-ah, was in 1951 set aside as a day of mourning for the victims of the Holocaust by the Knesset (the Israeli Parliament). The Central Conference of American Rabbis in June 1977 called for the annual commemoration of Yom HaSho-ah on this date.[225]

Anti-Semitism and Nazism did not die with the end of World War II. The *Sho-ah* is a constant reminder of the potential for evil which lies below the veneer of civilization. The seeds of the Holocaust must not be allowed to find fertile soil again.

It is a *mitzvah* to remember the six million Jews who were murdered in the *Sho-ah* by attending special memorial services. With them we should also remember *Chasidei Umot Ha-olam*, the righteous non-Jews who gave their lives in attempts to save members of the Jewish people.

In order to fulfill the *mitzvah* of remembrance, it is suggested that a memorial candle be lit and passages found in *Gates of Prayer* (pages 407–411) be read. Either as preparation or as part of the observance, one should spend time reviewing the events which led to the *Sho-ah* and discussing ways of preventing its recurrence.

In keeping with the spirit of Yom HaSho-ah as a day of mourning, weddings should not be scheduled. It is further suggested that one eat a very simple meal on the eve of Yom HaSho-ah as an act of identification and solidarity with those who were in the concentration camps and slowly starved to death. Particularly important is providing for a permanent memorial to the *Kedoshim*, the holy ones who perished. Therefore, our *Tzedakah* on Yom HaSho-ah should be directed to institutions which preserve their memory.

D.   *TISH-AH BE-AV (NINTH OF AV)*

TISH-AH Be-Av (the 9th of Av) has been the traditional day of mourning which commemorates major tragic events of the past— the destruction of the First Temple by the Babylonians in 587 B.C.E. and of the Second Temple by the Romans in 70 C.E.,[226] and the expulsion from Spain in 1492. Tradition has assigned additional subsequent major tragedies to the ninth of Av.[227] The day's special liturgy which has developed from the Biblical Book of Lamentations recalls the pain and suffering of the Jewish people.

Although many Jews have abandoned Tish-ah Be-Av, in part because of the re-establishment of the State of Israel, others continue to observe it by attending special services and/or by fasting. The Reform Movement has provided a liturgy for Tish-ah Be-Av, the text of which can be found in *Gates of Prayer*, page 573. These services are intended to memorialize all Jews who died *Al Kiddush HaShem*, "for the sanctification of God's name."

It is suggested that weddings not be scheduled for Tish-ah Be-Av. Reform Jews do not, however, observe the traditional strictures of avoiding weddings during certain periods before Tish-ah Be-Av.

E.   OTHERS

E-1   Tu BiShevat

The fifteenth day of Shevat (*Chamisha Asar BiShevat* or *Tu BiShevat*)[228] is designated by the Mishnah as the New Year for Trees. While it is a minor holiday without many prescribed observances, it is customary to eat fruits grown in Israel, especially the fruit of the carob tree (*bokser*). Among the Kabbalists, a *Seder* modeled on Pesach developed.[229]

Since the resettling of Israel, the day has been observed as a time for planting trees as a part of the reclamation of the land. Many Reform religious schools arrange special programs aimed at raising funds for the Jewish National Fund, and celebrating the gradual awakening of the land from the grip of winter. Because there are no special *mitzvot* associated with Tu BiShevat, its observances vary from place to place and new celebrations are emerging.

E-2   Fast Days

In addition to Yom Kippur and Tish-ah Be-Av there are four fast days mentioned in the *Tanach*[230]—the Fast of

Esther,[231] the Seventeenth of Tamuz,[232] the Tenth of Tevet,[233] and the Fast of Gedaliah.[234] Unlike Yom Kippur and Tishah Be-Av, fasting is limited to daylight hours. Reform Judaism takes no special note of these days in its liturgy and, in general, Reform Jews do not observe them.

E-3   Yom Yerushalayim

Yom Yerushalayim (Jerusalem Day) is celebrated on the twenty-eighth day of Iyar. On that date during the Six-Day War in June 1967, the Israeli Defense Forces captured Jerusalem and it once again became a united city. In the State of Israel, special prayers are added to the daily service. Some communities outside of Israel also mark the day with observances which focus on the meaning of Jerusalem in Jewish history.

Notes

Sources and Explanations

THE CYCLE OF THE JEWISH YEAR

[1] In the Hebrew calendar, the days of the week do not have names, but are numbered according to their relationship to Shabbat—Sunday is *Yom Rishon leShabbat*, "the first day toward Shabbat;" Monday is *Yom Sheni leShabbat*, "the second day toward Shabbat"; etc.

Shabbat is unique among the holy days, because it is independent of the cyclical changes of nature. "Since the rhythm of the Sabbath is the only exception to the prevailing natural rhythm and since the exception in no way derives from time as such nor is traceable to any aspect of time experienced in the ancient Near East, it is likely that the opposition between the Sabbath on one hand and nature on the other hand was not unintentional. The intention was, I suggest, to fill time with a contact that is uncontaminated by, and distinct from anything related to natural time, i.e., time as agricultural season or astronomical phase . . . that content, displacing the various ideas and phenomena associated with natural time is the idea of the absolute sovereignty of God, a sovereignty unqualified even by an indirect cognizance of the rule of other powers. As man takes heed of the Sabbath day and keeps it holy, he not only relinquishes the opportunity of using part of his time as he pleases but also forgoes the option of tying it to the secure and beneficial order of nature" (Matitiahu Tsevat, "The Meaning of the Sabbath," *The Meaning of the Book of Job and Other Biblical Studies* [New York: KTAV, 1980], pages 50–52).

[2] Mishnah, *Avot* 4.2.

THE JEWISH CALENDAR

[3] Talmud B., *Sanhedrin* 11ab.

[4] *Ibid.*, 12a.

[5] Genesis 1:5, "And there was evening and there was morning, one day."

[6] To determine if a given year is a leap year, one divides the date by 19, and if the remainder is 0, 3, 6, 8, 11, 14, or 17, it is a leap year.

[7] It should be noted that the names Kislev, Tevet, Adar, Nisan, Sivan, and Elul are found only in the books of Zechariah, Nehemiah, and Esther, all of which were written after the Babylonian exile.

[8] Talmud, *ibid.*, 97b; B. *Avodah Zarah* 9b.

[9] Mishnah, *Rosh Hashanah* 2.2.

[10] Talmud Yer., *Rosh Hashanah* 2.1, 58a.

[11] Mishnah, *Rosh Hashanah* 2.7.

[12] S. Zeitlin, "The Second Day of the Holidays in the Diaspora and the Second Day of Rosh Ha-Shanah in Israel," *CCAR Journal*, April 1969, pages 48–57.

[13] Talmud Yer., *Pesachim* 4.1, 30d.

[14] W. G. Plaut, *The Rise of Reform Judaism* (New York: World Union for Progressive Judaism, 1963), pages 195–198.

[15] Alexander Guttmann, *Rabbinic Judaism in the Making* (Detroit: Wayne State University Press, 1970), pages 175 and 277 (note 363).

[16] S. R. Hirsch, *Betrachtungen zum jüdische Kalendarjahr* (*Gesammelte Schriften*), 1:1.

EVERY DAY

[17] *Gates of Mitzvah*, page 38, E-3, and notes 68 and 69 on page 83. Daily services may be found in *Gates of Prayer*, pages 31–114, and *Gates of the House*, pages 133–203. Also, morning and evening prayers may be found in *Gates of the House*, pages 3–5. Private prayer is an important part of daily living. However, in some congregations there is a daily service which provides the opportunity to fulfill the *mitzvah* with other members of the community.

[18] *Gates of Mitzvah*, pages 40–41, E-7. The text of table blessings may be found in *Gates of the House*, pages 6–18.

[19] *Gates of Mitzvah*, page 19, E-1, and page 22, F-1.

[20] The *mitzvah* of honoring one's parents is found in both versions of the Ten Commandments (Exodus 20:12 and Deuteronomy 5:16).

[21] Leviticus 19, which is part of a section known as the Holiness Code, is a rich source of *mitzvot* which define relationships among human beings.

For example, "You shall not falsify measures of length, weight or capacity. You shall have an honest balance, honest weights, an honest *eifa* and honest *hin*" (Leviticus 19:35–36).

[22] Leviticus 19:18, "You shall love your neighbor as yourself."

[23] Leviticus 19:15, "You shall not render an unfair decision; do not favor the poor or show deference to the rich; judge your neighbor fairly."

[24] For example, Amos 5:21–24: "I loathe, I spurn your festivals, I am not appeased by your solemn assemblies. If you offer Me burnt offerings or your meal offerings I will not accept them. I will pay no heed to your gifts of fatlings. Spare Me the sound of your hymns, and let Me not hear the music of your lutes. But let justice well up like water, righteousness like an unfailing stream."

[25] *Avot deRabbi Natan*, chapter 15.

SHABBAT

[26] As quoted in *Gates of Prayer*, page 191, deriving from Achad Ha-am's "Shabbat Vetsiyonut," *Hashiloach* III, 6 (1898), reprinted in *Al Parashat Derachim* (Tel Aviv: 1955), page 496.

[27] "For in six days the Lord made heaven and earth and sea, and all that is in them, and God rested on the seventh day; therefore the Lord blessed Shabbat day and hallowed it" (Exodus 20:11).

[28] "Remember that you were a slave in the land of Egypt and the Lord your God freed you from there with a mighty hand and an outstreched arm; therefore the Lord your God has commanded you to observe Shabbat day" (Deuteronomy 5:15).

[29] *Gates of Prayer*, page 719, "With love and favor God has made the holy Shabbat, as a reminder of the work of creation."

[30] *Ibid.*, "It is the first among our sacred days and a remembrance of the Exodus from Egypt."

[31] According to Rabbinic legend, an additional soul (*Neshamah Yeterah*) dwells in the Jew during Shabbat (Talmud B., *Beitsah* 16a, and *Taanit* 27b).

[32] Mishnah, *Tamid* 7.4, and Talmud B., *Rosh Hashanah* 31a.

[33] Exodus 20:8 and Deuteronomy 5:12.

[34] The Talmud (B., *Ketubot* 62b) designates Friday night as the appropriate time for scholars and their wives to have sexual intercourse. Rashi in his commentary explains that the reason for the injunction is that Shabbat is a time of "pleasure, rest, and physical enjoyment." Furthermore, a 13th-century Kabbalistic text, *Igeret Hakodesh*, views sexual intercourse as being in keeping with the spiritual nature of Shabbat (*The Holy Letter* [New York: KTAV, 1976], pages 66–79). The *Shulchan Aruch, Orach Chayim* 280.1, adds: "Sexual relations are one of Shabbat's joys."

[35] "And on the seventh day God finished the work He had been doing, and ceased on the seventh day from all the work which He had done. And God blessed the seventh day and declared it holy because on it God ceased from all the work of creation which He had done" (Genesis 2:2–3). We should be aware that the original meaning of the Hebrew word *kadosh* ("holy") is "to be set aside or apart as special." It is only when Shabbat is in fact different from the other days of the week that we can say it is *kadosh* ("holy") for us.

[36] According to Rabbinic lore, the world was still incomplete on the sixth day. "What did the world lack? It lacked *Menuchah* (rest). Shabbat came and rest came and the world was now complete" (Rashi's commentary to Genesis 2:2, and Talmud B., *Megilah* 6a). The Midrash (*Genesis Rabbah* 10.9) adds that tranquility, ease, peace, and quiet were created on the first Shabbat. *Menuchah* is a positive concept which required a special act of creation. Each Shabbat, the individual has the opportunity to experience *Menuchah* which refreshes both body and spirit.

[37] Talmud B., *Shabbat* 113b: "Your conversation on Shabbat shall not be like your conversation on weekdays." Rashi comments that one should not discuss business on Shabbat. In order to experience the tranquility which Shabbat can bring, one should refrain from discussing those things which will deflect one's attention from the special character of Shabbat.

[38] *Ibid.*, 113a: "Your walking on Shabbat shall not be like your walking on weekday." On Shabbat there is no need to hurry. By walking more

slowly one adds to the restfulness of the day. Everything is slower on Shabbat because there is plenty of time. It is a day of being rather than a day of doing.

[39] The Midrash (*Genesis Rabbah* 17.5; 44.17) and the Talmud (B., *Berachot* 57b) describe Shabbat as a reflection of the world to come. Shabbat's ability to transform the world from the real to the ideal, even for just a little while, fills the Jew with new hope and new resolve.

[40] The Mishnah (*Shabbat* 7.2) lists thirty-nine classes of activities which are to be categorized as work and prohibited on Shabbat. The Talmud, Codes, and Responsa literature have elaborated and refined this list. While there are some Jews who choose to define work in accord with these definitions, many no longer consider certain prohibited activities as work. A renewal of Shabbat observance requires a new definition of work and rest. An attempt at such a definition is to be found in the essay "Shabbat as Protest," pages 145–146. This book affirms the principle that a Jew should not work on Shabbat. A person's gainful occupation is classified as work and should not be engaged in on Shabbat. All other activities must be judged in light of the way they contribute to or detract from Shabbat as a day of *Oneg* (joy), *Menuchah* (rest), and *Kedushah* (holiness). This means that there may be a wide variation in the specific activities that individual Jews will do and refrain from doing on Shabbat. Such a rethinking of the definitions of work and rest will make it possible for many to reconsider their own observance and return to Shabbat.

[41] The Talmud (B., *Beitsah* 9ab) discusses actions which are not actual violations of Shabbat or the festivals but which give the appearance of a violation. This is called *mar-it ayin* (appearance of the eye). This concept should sensitize Jews to the need to make sure that their public posture is one of respect for Shabbat observance.

[42] In the *Mechilta* (*Bachodesh* VII, ed. Lauterbach, pages 252–253): "Eleazar b. Chananiah b. Chezekiah b. Garon says, 'Remember the Sabbath day to keep it holy.' Keep it in mind from the first day of the week on, so if something good happens to come your way, prepare it for Shabbat."

[43] The Talmud (B., *Beitsah* 16a) records the practice of Shammai the Elder who always sought the choicest food for the Shabbat table. If earlier

in the week he found a particularly fine animal, he set it aside for Shabbat, and if later in the week he found a better animal, he would eat the first and set aside the second. In this manner he prepared for Shabbat. Today one may follow his example by planning the Shabbat meal to include something special; for example: the first fruit of the new season, or even a fruit out of season, a particularly choice cut of meat, or any dish which those gathered at the table would find especially enjoyable.

44 The Talmud (B., *Shabbat* 113a) states: "Your Shabbat garments should not be like your weekday garments." Dressing up for Shabbat adds to its festive character and distinguishes it from the other days of the week. If during the week one purchases a new garment which is appropriate for Shabbat, then waiting to wear it for the first time on Shabbat can contribute to one's enjoyment of Shabbat.

45 The Talmud (*ibid.*, 119a) compares Shabbat to a bride or queen. Almost all of the specifics of Shabbat preparation can be derived from the concept of Shabbat as an important guest.

46 The Talmud (*ibid.*) describes the individual preparations of the Sages. Their personal involvement included chopping wood and cooking the meal. The *Shulchan Aruch* (*Orach Chayim* 250.1) emphasizes the need for each individual to participate by stating that even those who have servants should assume some of the tasks of preparation.

47 The Talmud (*Shabbat* 127a), elaborating on the Mishnah (*Pe-ah* 1.1), lists *Hachnasat Orechim* among those *mitzvot* for which "a person is rewarded in this world and in the world to come." One does not have to believe in physical reward and punishment to accept the idea that the performance of *Hachnasat Orechim* (and the other humanitarian *mitzvot* on this list; see also *Gates of Prayer*, page 285) is eternally rewarding.

   In the same Talmudic passage, Rabbi Judah went even further in praise of *Hachnasat Orechim*, teaching that "welcoming guests is of greater merit even than welcoming the presence of God." Today, considering the great number of fragmented families and single adults in our society (see *Gates of Mitzvah*, "The Single Person, the Single-Parent Family, and *Mitzvot*," page 119) and the particular difficulty that such people have in observing home-centered *mitzvot*, it is of the greatest importance to invite them into the family circle and to include them in *Chavurot* (congregational subgroups which meet to study Judaism and/or celebrate Shabbat and festivals).

[48] The *mitzvah* of *Tzedakah* has its roots in the Biblical injunction, "You shall surely open your hand to your poor and needy kin" (Deuteronomy 15:11). Maimonides (*Sefer Hamitzvah, Mitzvot Aseh* #195) states that this means "we are to help our poor and support them according to their needs." In Jewish tradition, holy days and life-cycle events provide additional opportunities to perform this *mitzvah*.

[49] For example, every Friday afternoon R. Chaninah would send four *zuzim* to the poor (Talmud B., *Ketubot* 64a).

[50] The Talmud (B., *Shabbat* 25b) states explicitly that the kindling of Shabbat lights is a *mitzvah*, and it is clear that by Mishnaic times it was already a well-established practice (Mishnah, *Shabbat* 2.6,7). The Midrash (*Tanchuma, Noach* 1) connects the lighting of Shabbat lights with the concept of Shabbat joy (*Oneg*): " 'And you shall call Shabbat a joy' (Isaiah 58:12). This is kindling the lights on Shabbat."

[51] Usually when one performs a *mitzvah* which requires the recitation of a blessing, one recites the blessing and then performs the *mitzvah*, e.g., *Kiddush*—the blessing is recited first and then the wine is drunk. However, the lighting of Shabbat candles requires a different procedure. Since the recitation of the blessing marks the formal beginning of Shabbat, and since according to the traditional definition of work the lighting of a fire on Shabbat is prohibited, one first lights the candles and then covers one's eyes and recites the blessing.

[52] While the lighting of candles is more closely associated with women, men are also responsible for performing the *mitzvah* (*Yad, Hilchot Shabbat* 5.2).

[53] Jewish calendars which are printed each year specify the traditional time for lighting candles as 18 minutes before sunset. This is to assure that they are lit before the beginning of Shabbat.

[54] *Gates of Prayer*, page 189.

[55] *Shulchan Aruch, Orach Chayim* 263.1.

[56] Exodus 20:8; Deuteronomy 5:12.

[57] The custom of lighting candles and reciting *Kiddush* in the synagogue

stems from the time when the synagogue served as a lodging place for travelers (Talmud B., *Pesachim* 101a).

[58] In the *Mechilta* (*Bachodesh* VII, ed. Lauterbach, page 253), the *mitzvah* of *Kiddush* is derived from Exodus 20:8: " 'To keep it holy' means to hallow it with a benediction. On the basis of this passage the Sages said: At the beginning of the Sabbath we hallow it by reciting the *Kiddush* (sanctification) over wine." (Also Talmud B., *Pesachim* 106a).

The *Kiddush* consists of two blessings: the blessing over the wine and the blessing over the day. If one does not have wine for *Kiddush*, then one may substitute bread for wine and recite *Hamotsi* followed by the blessing over the day.

[59] See note 57 above.

[60] *Gates of Mitzvah*, pages 41–42, E-9, and note 77 on page 85.

[61] J. Hertz, *Authorized Daily Prayerbook*, page 977.

[62] Mishnah, *Berachot* 6.1.

[63] The two *Challot*, known as *Lechem Mishneh*, correspond to the double portion of manna which fell in the desert on the sixth day (Exodus 16:22).

[64] In Rabbinical writings, the family table is often compared to the Altar of the Temple. It is for this reason that the custom arose to sprinkle salt on the bread or *Challah* after *Hamotsi*, as we read in Leviticus 2:13: "You shall offer salt along with your sacrificed offerings."

[65] Interpreting Isaiah 58:13, "And you shall call Shabbat a joy," the Talmud (B., *Shabbat* 118b) asks: "In what does one express one's joy?" and proceeds to describe joy as eating food especially prepared for Shabbat. Jewish lore records many examples of the special character of the Shabbat meal throughout Jewish literature, e.g., food tasted better on Shabbat (Midrash, *Genesis Rabbah* 11.4; Talmud B., *Shabbat* 119a).

[66] Talmud B., *Shabbat* 113b.

[67] "You shall eat and be satisfied and bless the Lord your God ... " (Deuteronomy 8:10). See *Gates of Mitzvah*, pages 84–85, note 74.

[68] On the *mitzvah* of daily prayer, see *Gates of Mitzvah*, page 20, E-3, and page 38, E-3. While private prayer is a *mitzvah* and always desirable,

worship with a congregation is a *mitzvah* of superior importance. The Talmud (B., *Berachot* 6a) says:

> Rabin b. R. Adda says in the name of R. Isaac: How do you know that the Holy One, blessed be He, is to be found in the Synagogue? For it is said: "God stands in the congregation of God" (Psalm 82:1). And how do you know that if ten people pray together the Divine Presence is with them? For it is said: "God stands in the congregation of God" (*ibid.*).

[69] The "long" *Kiddush* is recited only at night (Talmud B., *Pesachim* 106b). The *Kiddush* for the Shabbat noon meal consists of "*Veshameru*" (Exodus 31:16–17) and the blessing over wine (*Shulchan Aruch, Orach Chayim* 289.1).

[70] *Gates of Mitzvah*, page 19, E-1; page 22, F-1, 2; note 26 on page 23.

[71] The Talmud (B., *Bava Kama* 82a) offers the following explanation for the origin of the public reading of Torah on Shabbat:

> "And they went three days in the wilderness and found no water" (Exodus 15:22), upon which those who expound verses metaphorically said: Water means nothing but Torah, as it says, "Ho, everyone that is thirsty come for water" (Isaiah 55:1). It thus means that as they went three days without Torah they immediately became exhausted. The prophets among them thereupon rose and enacted that they should publicly read the law on Sabbath, make a break on Sunday, read again on Monday, make a break again on Tuesday and Wednesday, read again on Thursday, and then make a break on Friday, so that they should not be kept for three days without Torah.

[72] For example, W. Gunther Plaut (ed.), *The Torah: A Modern Commentary* (New York: UAHC, 1981).

[73] *Gates of Mitzvah*, page 47, A-3; notes 87 and 88 on page 88.

[74] The Talmud (B., *Mo-ed Katan* 9a) prohibits marriage on a festival because one may not mix two joyous occasions ("*Ein me-arevin simchah besimchah*," i.e., a wedding is a *simchah* and the festival is a *simchah*). Further, the *Shulchan Aruch* (*Orach Chayim* 339.4 and *Even Ha-ezer* 64.3) states that marriages may not be performed on Shabbat and the Festivals. This prohibition is based on the Talmudic statement in B., *Beitsah* 36b and the underlying Mishnah (5.2). These prohibitions do not relate to biblically prohibited work, but were issued by the Rabbis in an effort to protect the sanctity of Shabbat.

The Responsa Committee of the CCAR (*CCAR Yearbook*, vol. XXXVII, pages 96–99) opposed the performance of marriages on Shabbat and festivals for the following reasons:

(1) Since the avoidance of weddings on Shabbat has the weight of a widely observed *minhag* which supports the spirit of Shabbat, it should not be dismissed or disregarded.

(2) The Reform movement has encouraged Shabbat observance in creative ways for more than a decade. We have published a *Shabbat Manual*, and we encourage our members to make this a "special day" upon which we do not carry out duties and acts performed on other days. Countenancing marriages on Shabbat would detract from this objective and weaken our efforts.

(3) We have a great respect for *Kelal Yisra-el* and wish to do everything possible to advance the unity of the Jewish people.

(4) Our tradition has always emphasized that in addition to all else, marriage has companionship, procreation, and family life as its basis, but there are also various economic aspects which form an important element of the traditional *Ketubah*, although these aspects are not stressed by Reform Jews. However, economic considerations do play a considerable role at a time when the family is about to be established in terms of property rights, insurance benefits, etc., and an equally large role when such a family is dissolved. These may not be readily apparent to the couple; although they may not be "transactions" in the ordinary sense, Shabbat is not the time to initiate them.

(5) We are opposed to the performance of marriages on Shabbat as we prefer allegiance to a hallowed tradition rather than mere convenience.

[75] While Shabbat is counted as part of the *Shiv-ah* (i.e., the first seven days of mourning), all formal mourning is suspended and the basic *mitzvot* of Shabbat are observed (Talmud B., *Mo-ed Katan* 19a and *Semachot* 7.1).

[76] Funerals are not conducted on Shabbat, nor on the first day or last day of a major festival, since no work may be performed, and the mood of the funeral is contrary to the spirit of rejoicing (*Oneg*) which characterizes Shabbat and the festivals.

[77] *Havdalah* was already a well-established practice in early Mishnaic times (Mishnah, *Berachot* 8.5; Tosefta, *Berachot* 6.7). The principal blessing, the blessing of *Havdalah* (separation), is mentioned in the Talmud (B., *Pesachim* 103b). A detailed explanation of, and sources for, *Havdalah* can be found in *Gates of Understanding*, pages 253–255.

Maimonides (*Yad, Hilchot Shabbat* 29.1) derives the *mitzvah* of *Havdalah* from Exodus 20:8: " 'Remember Shabbat to keep it holy.' ... It is obligatory to remember Shabbat both when it commences and when it terminates; by reciting *Kiddush* when it commences, and *Havdalah* when it terminates."

Shabbat terminates at sunset. It is customary to wait until one can see three stars in the sky. Many prefer to delay *Havdalah* as late as possible, thereby holding on to Shabbat as long as possible.

78 The Talmud (B., *Pesachim* 103a) stipulates that a torch be used for *Havdalah*. In the blessing over the light, the word for light—"*meorei*"—is plural; this has been interpreted to mean that the *Havdalah* candle must have two or more wicks.

ROSH HASHANAH

79 While the first of Tishri is designated by the Torah as "the day when the horn is sounded" (Numbers 29:1), it is the Mishnah (*Rosh Hashanah* 1.1) which first identifies it as the New Year. Not only is the first of Tishri the first day of New Year, but it is also the birthday of the world (Talmud B., *Rosh Hashanah* 11a). It is the complex interconnection of New Year, Creation, and Judgment, that provides the conceptual framework for understanding the *mitzvot* and customs of Rosh Hashanah.

80 According to the Mishnah (*ibid.*, 1.2), Rosh Hashanah is one of the four times during the year that the world is judged. The Tosefta (*ibid.*) conceives of judgment commencing on Rosh Hashanah, but the final verdict remains open until Yom Kippur. Therefore, the period between Rosh Hashanah and Yom Kippur became an especially appropriate time for self-examination and repentance.

81 The Midrash (*Pirkei deRabbi Eliezer* 46) identifies the first of Elul as the day on which Moses ascended Mt. Sinai to receive the second set of the Ten Commandments. Since Moses remained on the mountain for forty days, the Rabbis identified this whole period, from the first of Elul until Yom Kippur, as a period of penitential prayer and repentance.

Traditional Rabbinic exegesis considers the Song of Songs to be an allegorical description of God's love for Israel. The name of the month Elul consists of the four Hebrew letters *Alef, Lamed, Vav, Lamed*. These four letters were interpreted as referring to the first letters of the words in Song of Songs 6:3: *Ani Ledodi Vedodi Li*, "I am my beloved's and my beloved is mine." Therefore, Elul is the period of reconciliation between God and Israel.

[82] In Jewish tradition many reasons have been offered for the sounding of the *Shofar*: The ram's horn is identified with the ram which became the substitute sacrifice for Isaac (Genesis 22:1–19); the giving of the Torah at Sinai was accompanied by the sounding of the *Shofar* (Exodus 19:20); the proclamation of the Jubilee was heralded by the blast of the *Shofar* (Leviticus 24:9–11); and the commencement of Messianic times is to be announced by the sound of the great *Shofar* (Isaiah 27:13). Our liturgy (*Gates of Repentance*, page 139) cites Maimonides's call to awaken from our spiritual slumber:

> Awake, you sleepers, from your sleep! Rouse yourselves, you slumberers, out of your slumber! Examine your deeds, and turn to God in repentance. Remember your Creator, you who are caught up in the daily round, losing sight of eternal truth; you who are wasting your years in vain pursuits that neither profit nor save. Look closely at yourselves; improve your ways and your deeds. Abandon your evil ways, your unworthy schemes, every one of you! (*Yad, Hilchot Teshuva* 3.4).

[83] Talmud B., *Rosh Hashanah* 16b.

[84] In the Talmud (B., *Kiddushin* 40a,b) one finds the following:

> Our Rabbis taught: A man should regard himself as though he were half guilty and half meritorious—if he performs one precept, happy is he for weighting himself down in the scale of merit; if he commits one transgression, woe to him for weighting himself down in the scale of guilt, for it is said, "But one sinner destroys much good" (Kohelet 9:18), [i.e.], on account of a single sin which he commits much good is lost to him. R. Eleazar, son of R. Simeon, said: Because the world is judged by its majority, and an individual [too] is judged by his majority [of deeds, good or bad]—if he performs one good deed, happy is he for turning the scale both for himself and for the whole world on the side of merit; if he commits one transgression, woe to him for weighting himself and the whole world in the scale of guilt, for it is said, "but one sinner "[*ibid.*]; on account of the single sin which this man commits he and the whole world lose much good.

[85] Midrash *Bereshit Rabbah* 44.12. It is found in a slightly different version in Talmud B., *Rosh Hashanah* 16b, and in Rosh Hashanah liturgy (*Gates of Repentance*, page 109).

[86] *Deuteronomy Rabbah* 2.12. The Midrash (*Exodus Rabbah* 19.4) enlarges on the concept of God's openness to repentance in its exegesis of Job

31:32: " 'No stranger need lodge in the street.' The Holy one, blessed be He, does not reject a single creature. Rather, all are acceptable to God. The gates are open at all times and all who wish may enter."

[87] See note 81 above.

[88] The word *selichot* is the plural form of the Hebrew word *selicha*, which means forgiveness. Since most Reform congregations do not have daily services, *Selichot* are only recited late on the Saturday night before Rosh Hashanah (see "Fragments of Faith: On Holy Day Liturgy," pages 147–153).

[89] If Rosh Hashanah falls on a Monday or Tuesday, *Selichot* services are held on the Saturday night of the previous week (*Rama* on *Orach Chayim* 581.1).

[90] The custom of blowing the *Shofar* from the first of Elul is based on the same Midrashic passage from *Pirkei deRabbi Eliezer* cited in note 81 above. The *Shofar* is not sounded on the day before Rosh Hashanah in order to make a distinction between the end of Elul and Rosh Hashanah.

[91] *Rama* on *Orach Chayim* 581.4.

[92] See note 80 above.

[93] See note 83 above.

[94] There is a custom called *Tashlich* of going to a body of water on the afternoon of Rosh Hashanah and symbolically casting out one's sins. See J. Z. Lauterbach, *Rabbinic Essays* (Cincinnati: Hebrew Union College Press, 1951), page 432, for summary of its history. While *Tashlich* is not practiced by the majority of Reform congregations, there are some who have instituted it as part of their Rosh Hashanah observance.

[95] See "Shabbat," A-11, page 25, and "Shabbat," note 48, on page 115. The practice of giving *Tzedakah* on Erev Rosh Hashanah is mentioned in the *Rama* on *Orach Chayim* 581.4.

[96] Rosh Hashanah is included in Leviticus 23 along with Shabbat, Pesach, Shavuot, Yom Kippur, Sukkot, and Atseret/Simchat Torah as major festivals. The *Mechilta* (*Bachodesh* VII, ed. Lauterbach, vol. II, page 253) links the Shabbat *Kiddush* and the Festival *Kiddush* on the basis of Leviticus 23:4: "These are the festivals of the Lord." Maimonides (*Yad, Hilchot Shabbat* 29.18) states: "Just as *Kiddush* is said on Friday

night and *Havdalah* at the termination of the Sabbath, so also is *Kiddush* recited on the night of a festival and *Havdalah* at the termination of the festival and Yom Kippur, for all these are 'Sabbaths of the Lord' (Leviticus 23:38)." The lighting of candles is also based on this analogy.

[97] Customs vary as to the shape of the *Challot* for Rosh Hashanah. In some places round *Challot* with raisins signifying a full and sweet year are used, and in other places *Challot* in the form of a ladder symbolically reaching toward heaven are used.

[98] See above, "Shabbat," A-18, page 30, and note 68 on page 116 above.

[99] It is a common Reform practice to blow the *Shofar* on Rosh Hashanah even when it falls on Shabbat. Conservative and Orthodox congregations, however, following the ruling of the *Shulchan Aruch* (*Orach Chayim* 588.5), do not sound the *Shofar* on the first day of Rosh Hashanah when it falls on Shabbat. In such a case they sound it only on the second day, which can never fall on Shabbat. The reasons for current Reform practice are discussed in the *CCAR Yearbook*, vol. XXIII, pages 182–183 and vol. XXXIII, pages 60–61, and by Solomon B. Freehof in *Recent Reform Responsa*, pages 36–41. At the end of his discussion, Rabbi Freehof summarizes the matter as follows (pages 40–41): "Since the sounding of the shofar on the Sabbath is not really prohibited in itself, since the sounding of the shofar on the New Year is a Biblical mandate, and since some authorities at least permitted the shofar to be sounded on the New Year Sabbath even though the people would have heard it on the second day anyway, we, who observe only one day [see A-12 below, page 43], should not, in my judgment, deprive our people of the spiritual benefit of hearing the sound of the shofar when the New Year comes on the Sabbath."

[100] See note 82 above.

[101] Essential to the fulfillment of this *mitzvah* is the concept of *Kavanah*, the directing of one's mind toward the meaning and significance of the sounding of the *Shofar* (Mishnah, *Rosh Hashanah* 3.7, and Talmud B., *Rosh Hashanah* 28b, where the Mishnah is discussed).

[102] Talmud B., *Mo-ed Katan* 19a, and Mishnah, *Semachot* 7.1.

[103] See note 96 above.

TEN DAYS OF REPENTANCE

[104] The Talmud (B., *Rosh Hashanah* 18a) designates the period from Rosh Hashanah to Yom Kippur as being a particularly propitious time for repentance: " 'Seek the Lord while He may be found' (Isaiah 55:6). Where can the individual find God? Rabba b. Abuha replied, 'These are the ten days from Rosh Hashanah to Yom Kippur.' "

[105] Complete repentance, according to the Talmud (B., *Yoma* 86b), involves having both the ability and opportunity to repeat a sin for which one has repented and to refrain from repeating it. In addition, one must make restitution and seek the forgiveness of the agrieved persons (Mishnah, *Bava Kama* 9.7).

[106] Mishnah, *Yoma* 8.9. See also note 109 below.

[107] The Talmudic concept of repentance involves the explicit confession of sins (B., *Yoma* 36b, 86b). Such a process requires a careful review of our behavior in order to determine where we have failed to live up to the standards which we set for ourselves and which are derived from the *mitzvot* of Jewish living.

[108] Mishnah, *ibid.*

[109] Seeking forgiveness and being forgiving is part of the Talmudic understanding of the process of repentance (Mishnah, *Bava Kama* 9.7). Maimonides, in his code (*Yad, Hilchot Teshuvah* 2.8–9), basing himself on Leviticus 19:18, "Do not bear a grudge and do not take vengence," considers the one who is unwilling to forgive as a sinner. The duality of this procedure is a recognition of the potential destructiveness of unresolved conflict as well as the power of repentance to rebuild relationships, renew the individual, and strengthen the community.

[110] Talmud B., *Ta-anit* 20a.

[111] *Shulchan Aruch, Orach Chayim* 581.4.

YOM KIPPUR

[112] Only Shabbat (Exodus 31:15; 35:2, Leviticus 23:3) and Yom Kippur (Leviticus 16:31; 23:32) are called *Shabbat Shabbaton*, the Sabbath of Sabbaths.

[113] The Biblical formula which was recited by King Solomon (I Kings 8:47) is part of the *Vidui*, confessional prayers, of Yom Kippur (*Gates of Repentance*, pages 269, 324, and 512). For a discussion of the *Vidui*, see "Fragments of Faith: On Holy Day Liturgy," pages 147–153.

[114] According to the Mishnah (*Yoma* 8.8), Yom Kippur brings about atonement when accompanied by repentance.

[115] This concept of mutual turning is suggested in the statement of the prophet Malachi (3:7), "Return to Me and I will return to you, said the Lord of Hosts."

[116] See above, "Ten Days of Repentance," B–2, page 46. During the Ten Days of Repentance one should have made contact in person, by mail, or by telephone with all of the people one believes he/she may have offended. The dinner on Erev Yom Kippur should then be seen as a final opportunity to effect reconciliation with the family and friends who are gathered around the table.

[117] See above, "Shabbat," A–11, page 25; "Rosh Hashanah," A–4, page 40.

[118] The concept of *Kaparah* (means of expiation) is probably based on the ancient scapegoat ritual for Yom Kippur (Leviticus 16:5–22). In later times the custom of *Kaparot* (plural of *Kaparah*) developed. One day before Yom Kippur a person would swing a fowl around his/her head three times, and recite the formula: "This is my substitute, my vicarious offering, my atonement; this cock [or hen] shall meet death but I shall find a long and pleasant life of peace." The fowl was then slaughtered and given to the poor. There has been much Rabbinic opposition to this custom, and today it is practiced only among some Orthodox Jews. A variation of this rite was the substitution of money for the fowl. While Reform Jews do not practice the ritual of *Kaparot*, the basic connection between charity and repentance is integral to atonement and to the observance of Yom Kippur.

[119] The Talmud (B., *Yoma* 81b) enunciates the principle of adding ordinary time to sacred time in order to lengthen the observance of a festival or holy day. Therefore, it is customary to begin the final meal early.

[120] *Shulchan Aruch, Orach Chayim* 610.1–3.

[121] "*Ve-initem et nafshoteichem*, and you should practice self-denial" (Leviticus 23:27), is interpreted by the Mishnah (*Yoma* 8.1) to include not

only refraining from eating and drinking but also washing, anointing, sexual intercourse, and wearing leather shoes. The majority of Reform Jews understand "self-denial" as abstaining from eating and drinking only.

[122] Mishnah, *Yoma* 8.4, and Talmud B., *Yoma* 82a.

[123] The Mishnah (*Yoma* 8.5–6) and the Talmud (*ibid.*, 82a ff) give examples of people who should not fast. The general principle is that when there is danger to human life, the laws of Shabbat are suspended—not only for actual danger but even for possible danger. Since Yom Kippur is *Shabbat Shabbaton*, the Sabbath of Sabbaths, the principle applies to it as well (Talmud B., *Yoma* 84b). Obviously the same principle applies to the other festivals.

[124] See above, "Shabbat," A–18, page 30, and note 68 on page 116.

[125] *Yizkor* (literally, "May He remember") is the popular name of the special prayer prescribed in the liturgy for recitation on certain holy days, especially Yom Kippur, in memory of the dead. *Yizkor* as recited in the Ashkenazic congregation probably dates only from after the Crusades. *Yizkor* is recited in all Reform congregations on Yom Kippur and on the seventh day of Pesach, and in many congregations on Shavuot and Atseret/Simchat Torah as well. (For the text of the service, see *Gates of Repentance*, pages 477–494, and *Gates of Prayer*, pages 546–553.)

[126] See above, "Rosh Hashanah," note 96, page 121.

[127] The custom of making a symbolic start on the *Sukkah* at the conclusion of Yom Kippur is based on the principle, "If a *mitzvah* comes your way, perform it immediately" (*Mechilta Pischa* IX, ed. Lauterbach, page 74). The *Shulchan Aruch* (*Orach Chayim* 24.1) applies this principle to the building of the *Sukkah*.

[128] Kohelet 9:7. The Midrash (*Kohelet Rabbah* 9.7) applies this verse to Yom Kippur.

THE PILGRIMAGE FESTIVALS

[129] While Shemini Atseret is the eighth day of Sukkot, it is considered a separate festival by the Talmud (B., *Sukkot* 47a-b). Simchat Torah is the second day of Shemini Atseret. Since Reform Jews follow the

calendar of Israel, Shemini Atseret and Simchat Torah are celebrated on the same day (see "The Jewish Calendar," pages 7–11).

[130]Rejoicing (*Simchah*) on the Festivals is similar to joy (*Oneg*) and rest (*Menuchah*) on Shabbat (see "Shabbat," A–2, page 21, and A–4, page 22). Special meals, wine, new clothes, and Torah study are part of the joyous celebration of the Festivals (see Talmud B., *Pesachim* 109 and *Beitsah* 15b). However, the key to Festival rejoicing is the turning away from everyday activities to observe the *mitzvot* of the day.

[131] See above, "Rosh Hashanah," note 96, page 121.

[132] The tradition makes only a minor distinction between the prohibition against work on Shabbat and on the Festivals: "The Festivals differ from Shabbat only in the preparation of necessary food" (Mishnah, *Megilah* 1.5 and *Beitsah* 5.2). However, the basic principle is that no work should be done on the Festival which interfers with the joy or sanctity of the Festival (*Yad, Hilchot Yom Tov* 1.5 and *Shulchan Aruch, Orach Chayim* 195.1, 510.8).

[133] See above, "Shabbat," note 68 on page 116.

[134] The *mitzvah* of rejoicing on the Festival (see "The Pilgrimage Festivals," A–2, page 61, and note 130 above) is incompatible with the *mitzvah* of mourning. Since the observance of the Festival is a communal obligation, it takes precedence over the mourning which is an individual obligation; therefore, formal mourning is suspended for the duration of the Festival (Talmud B., *Mo-ed Katan* 14b).

[135] See above, "Shabbat," note 74, page 117.

[136] See above, "Rosh Hashanah," note 96, page 121.

PESACH

[137] There are four special Sabbaths (called "*Arba parashiyot*") that precede Pesach: *Shabbat Shekalim* (see below, "Purim," note 217 on page 138), *Shabbat Zachor* (see below, "Purim," note 209 on page 137), *Shabbat Parah,* and *Shabbat Hachodesh.*

Shabbat Parah recalls the purification ritual of the Red Heifer (*Parah Adumah*). The additional Torah reading in Numbers 19:1–22 describes

the ritual. The *Haftarah*, taken from Ezekiel 36:22–36, is an escha-
tological description of Israel's future purification. *Shabbat Parah* served
as a reminder that the *Pesach* (paschal sacrifice) had to be eaten in a
state of ritual purity.

Shabbat Hachodesh is the Shabbat immediately preceding the month
of Nisan. In addition to the weekly Torah portion, Exodus 12:1–20
is also read. It describes the arrival of Nisan and the preparations for
Pesach. *Shabbat Hachodesh* announces the arrival of Nisan and serves
as part of the preparation for Pesach.

Additionally, the Sabbath immediately preceding Pesach is known
as *Shabbat Hagadol* (the Great Sabbath). According to some authorities,
the name is derived from one of the verses in the *Haftarah* (Malachi
3:4–24), "Behold I will send you Elijah the prophet before the coming
of the great and terrible day of the Lord" (3:23). This *Haftarah* was
selected in accordance with the Talmudic statement, "In Nisan they
were delivered; in Nisan they will be delivered in the future" (B., *Rosh
Hashanah* 11b). Since the redemption from Egypt occurred in Nisan,
so the Messianic redemption will occur in Nisan. On *Shabbat Hagadol*
it was customary for the rabbi to instruct the people on the proper
observance of Pesach.

[138] The development of the historical Passover is explained in *The Torah:
A Modern Commentary* (New York: UAHC, 1980), pages 464–466.

[139] The principle which governs the narration of the Passover story is that
"one begins with degradation and rises to dignity" (Mishnah, *Pesachim*
10.4). Therefore, according to the Talmud (B., *Pesachim* 116b), Samuel
began the narration with the passage, "We were slaves to Pharaoh in
Egypt . . . " (*A Passover Haggadah*, page 34), giving primacy to the
notion of physical bondage. However, Samuel's contemporary, Rav,
began the narration with the passage, "For in the beginning our ancestors
were idolators . . . " (*A Passover Haggadah*, page 35), placing the
emphasis on spiritual rather than physical slavery. The Mishnah (*ibid.*),
however, proposes a third possibility, that the narrative should begin
with an exposition of Deuteronomy 26:5, "My father was a fugitive
Aramean . . . "(*A Passover Haggadah*, page 34), interpreting slavery as
social degradation. The present *Haggadah* contains all three passages,
making it clear that slavery has physical, ideological, and social com-
ponents.

[140] Mishnah, *Pesachim* 10.5; *A Passover Haggadah*, page 56.

[141] Midrash, *Exodus Rabbah* 21.10.

[142] "The fourteenth day of the month at evening" is understood as the eve of the fifteenth, because the Jewish day begins at sundown.

[143] According to the Talmud (B., *Pesachim* 35a), these are the only grains from which *Matzah* can be made, and therefore, strictly speaking, the only ones which are subject to the prohibition of leaven. While the tradition developed many complex rules concerning what may be eaten and what may not be eaten during Pesach, the basic principle is that all leaven and all products containing leaven are not to be eaten.

[144] When it became economically unfeasible to dispose of all one's leaven during Pesach, the Rabbis developed a legal fiction whereby one sold the leaven to a non-Jew with the understanding that it would be returned after Pesach. This method became especially important to Jews whose businesses involve the extensive use of leaven. Reform Jews rarely resort to this method and instead make leaven inaccessible in their homes.

[145] The Mishnah (*Pesachim* 1.1,3) sets forth the requirement to search for leaven on the night of the fourteenth of Nisan using a light to aid in the search.

[146] Maimonides, basing himself on the Mishnah (*Pesachim* 10.1), states that the Sages have forbidden the eating of *Matzah* on the eve of Pesach in order to make its eating at the *Seder* a distinct event. In addition, one should come to the *Seder* table hungry so that one may fully enjoy the *Seder* meal (*Yad, Hilchot Chamets Umatzah* 6.12).

[147] See above, "Shabbat," A-9, page 24. The changing of dishes for Pesach is a time-honored practice. While most Reform Jews do not change their dishes for Pesach, some have a separate set of dishes which are reserved for Pesach. Their use sets Pesach apart from the other days of the year.

[148] *A Passover Haggadah*, page 26. See above, "Shabbat," note 47, page 114.

[149] *Gates of Mitzvah*, pages 39–40, E-5, and "*Tzedakah*," pages 121–123.

[150] The name *Me-ot Chitin* means "money for wheat," indicating that originally the funds were collected so that the poor could buy *Matzah* for

Pesach. Already in Mishnaic times special provisions were made so that even the poor could celebrate Pesach properly (Mishnah, *Pesachim* 10.1).

[151] The yearly recitation at the *Seder* of the Pesach story is derived from the Rabbinic understanding of Exodus 13:8, "You shall explain to your child on that day, it is because of what the Lord did for me when I myself went forth from Egypt" (*Mechilta Pischa* III, ed. Lauterbach, page 149). The *Haggadah* itself reminds us that "even if all of us were wise, all of us people of understanding, all of us learned in Torah, it would still be our obligation to tell the story of the Exodus from Egypt" (*A Passover Haggadah*, page 34).

[152] Mishnah, *Pesachim* 10.5, based on Exodus 13:8; *A Passover Haggadah*, page 56.

[153] *Shulchan Aruch, Orach Chayim* 473.4. *A Passover Haggadah*, page 15, lists all the items to be included on the *Seder* Plate.

[154] Four cups of wine are required for the *Seder* (see below, "Pesach," B-13, page 72). However, there is a controversy among the Rabbis concerning the drinking of a fifth cup (Talmud B., *Pesachim* 118a; *Yad, Hilchot Chamets Umatzah* 8.10). Therefore, the cup was filled but not drunk. Since in the future Elijah was supposed to solve all legal controversies (Mishnah, *Eduyot* 8.7; Tosefta, *Eduyot* 3.4), the cup became associated with him and became known as Elijah's cup (*Kos Shel Eliyahu*).

Later the custom became associated with the belief that Elijah did not die but ascended to heaven alive (II Kings 2:11) and that he returned to earth from time to time to befriend the helpless, and in the future he would announce the coming of the Messiah (Malachi 3:23; *Pirkei DeR. Eliezer* 43). Further, it was believed that as the first redemption took place in Nisan, so the future redemption would take place in Nisan (Talmud B., *Rosh Hashanah* 11b). So the popular notion arose that a cup should be placed on the table to welcome the prophet as he visits each *Seder*.

[155] During the rest of the week the eating of *Matzah* is optional (Talmud B., *Pesachim* 120a). Although *Matzah* need not be eaten, one still abstains from eating leaven throughout Pesach (see above, "Pesach," B-3, page 68).

[156] *A Passover Haggadah*, page 55, based on Exodus 12:39.

[157] According to the Torah (Numbers 9:11), the Passover sacrifice was to be eaten with unleavened bread and bitter herbs.

[158] *A Passover Haggadah*, page 56, based on Exodus 1:14.

[159] The Mishnah (*Pesachim* 10.1) stipulates that even the poorest Jew be given no less than four cups of wine for the *Seder*. The Talmud (Yer., *Pesachim* 10.1, 37bc) relates the four cups to the four promises of redemption in Exodus 6:6–7: *Vehotseti*, "I will bring you out"; *vehitsalti*, "I will save you"; *vega-alti*, "I will redeem you"; *velakachti*, "I will take you." It also suggests that they are allusions to the four kingdoms mentioned in Daniel 7, or to the four cups of punishment poured out against Pharaoh which will be matched in the future with four cups of comfort for Israel.

The four cups correspond to four parts of the *Seder*: *Kiddush* and the blessing of redemption before the meal, and *Birkat Hamazon* and *Birkat Hashir* after the meal ("Blessing of the Song," also called "*Nishmat*"; *A Passover Haggadah*, pages 22–25, 60, 67, 75, 93).

[160] See note 159 above. There is a fifth promise of redemption (Exodus 6:8): *heveti*, "I will bring [you into the land]." The fifth cup remains optional (*Yad, Hilchot Chamets Umatzah* 8:10). *A Passover Haggadah*, pages 77–79, gives a series of readings for the fifth cup.

[161] Mishnah, *Pesachim* 10.4. The current *Haggadah* has a different version of the four questions. While contemporary *Haggadot* have a set formula for the four questions, spontaneity is to be encouraged. As Maimonides writes, "One should make some changes in procedures on this night of the fifteenth of Nisan in order that one's children will notice and ask, 'What makes this night different from other nights?'—to which one replies, 'This and this is what happened and this and this is what took place' " (*Yad, Hilchot Chamets Umatzah* 7.5).

[162] Mishnah, *Pesachim* 10.1.

[163] The middle *Matzah* is broken in two and set aside. This is called the *Afikoman*. The word *Afikoman* is of Greek origin, but its etymology is problematic. It has been variously interpreted to mean either "aftermeal entertainment" or "a dessert." The Mishnah (*Pesachim* 10.8) states: "One may not add *Afikoman* after the paschal meal." The Talmud (B., *Pesachim* 119b–120a) understands this to mean that the last food which is to be eaten at the *Seder* is the paschal lamb. However, since the

destruction of the Temple the *Afikoman* has become a symbolic reminder of the sacrifice, and one concludes the *Seder* with a piece of
Afikoman.

[164] Exodus 12:15 specifies that *Chamets* may not be eaten during the entire
seven days.

[165] The five small Biblical books—Song of Songs, Ruth, Lamentations,
Kohelet (Ecclesiastes), and Esther—are known as the Five Scrolls (*Cha-
mesh Megilot*). Each scroll is read on a particular festival or holy day:
Song of Songs on the intermediate Shabbat of Pesach; Ruth on Shavuot;
Lamentations on Tish-ah Be-Av; Kohelet on the intermediate Shabbat
of Sukkot; and Esther on Purim.

The custom of reading Song of Songs in connection with Pesach and
Ruth in connection with Shavuot is mentioned in *Soferim* 14.16, while
the custom of reading Kohelet in connection with Sukkot apparently
developed later.

[166] See above, "Yom Kippur," C–10, page 54, and note 125.

SHAVUOT

[167] The Biblical verse (Leviticus 23:15) states that the counting of the fifty-
day period from Pesach until Shavuot begins on the day after the
Sabbath. According to the Talmud (B., *Menachot* 65 ab), the Sadducees
(Boethusians) took the word Sabbath literally and began to count the
day after the Sabbath which occurred during Pesach, which meant that
the date of Shavuot varied from year to year. However, the Pharisees
understood the word Sabbath to refer to the first day of Pesach and
therefore began the counting on the second day of Pesach, thus estab-
lishing a fixed date for Shavuot.

Although the date of Shavuot is fixed, and although the wave offering
can no longer be practiced because of the destruction of the Temple
in Jerusalem (70 C.E.), the period between Pesach and Shavuot is still
known as *Sefirah*, "counting," or *Sefirat Ha-omer*, "counting the wave
offering." In Orthodox and Conservative synagogues the following blessing is recited from the second night of Pesach until the eve of Shabbat
at the end of the evening service (*Ma-ariv*):

Ba-ruch a-ta A-do-nai E-lo-hei-nu, me-lech ha-o-lam, a-sher ki-de-sha-nu be-mits-vo-tav ve-tsi-va-nu al se-fi-rat ha-o-mer.

Blessed is the Lord our God, Ruler of the Universe, Who hallows us with His Mitzvot and commanded us concerning the counting of the Omer.

This blessing is followed by the actual counting; for example: "This is the eighth day, making one week and one day of counting the *Omer.*"

Traditionally *Sefirah* is considered a period of semi-mourning because, according to the Talmudic tradition (B., *Yevamot* 62b), twelve thousand of Rabbi Akiba's disciples were killed between Pesach and Shavuot during the Hadrianic persecution which followed the Bar Kochba revolt (c.135 C.E.). While the majority of Reform congregations take no special note of this period, a few have revived the old custom of counting the days between Pesach and Shavuot.

Orthodox rabbis will not officiate at weddings during most of this period with the exception of *Lag Ba-omer* (thirty-third day of the *Omer*), Rosh Chodesh (New Month), and the last three days of the counting. While most Reform rabbis will perform weddings during this period, in seeking a wedding date the rabbi should be consulted (see *Gates of Mitzvah*, page 31, B-2). It is also recommended that weddings not be scheduled for Yom HaSho-ah (Holocaust Day) which falls during this period (see "Yom HaSho-ah," pages 102–103).

[168] Talmud B., *Shabbat* 86b.

[169] Exodus 24:7.

[170] See note 167 above.

[171] This custom has probably developed from Shavuot's association with the harvest (Exodus 23:16) and the first fruits (Exodus 34:22). The Mishnah (*Rosh Hashanah* 1.2) and the Talmud (B., *Rosh Hashanah* 16a) identify Shavuot as the time when God blesses the fruit of the tree.

[172] See note 168 above. Jewish tradition considers the *mitzvah* of *Talmud Torah* (Torah study) to be of overarching significance:

> These are the obligations without measure, whose reward, too, is without measure:
> To honor father and mother; to perform acts of love and kindness; to attend the
> house of study daily; to welcome the stranger; to visit the sick; to rejoice with

bride and groom; to console the bereaved; to pray with sincerity; to make peace when there is strife. And the study of Torah is equal to them all, because it leads to them all (Talmud B., *Shabbat* 127a, as cited in *Gates of Prayer*, page 185).

The study of Torah is not merely intellectual expertise but the means to discover how to live. Torah study leads the Jew to live a life of holiness.

[173] Solomon Alkabetz and his circle of 16th-century Kabbalists developed the custom in Salonica, and Alkabetz subsequently introduced it wherever he lived (R. J. Wesblowsky, *Joseph Karo: Lawyer and Mystic* [Oxford, 1962], pages 109–110).

[174] Solomon B. Freehof, *Reform Jewish Practice* I (New York:UAHC, 1964), pages 25–26; *CCAR Resolutions*, page 11. It should be noted that some Reform congregations hold Confirmation on the Shabbat nearest Shavuot rather than on Shavuot itself.

[175] See above, "Pesach," note 165.

[176] *Abudarham Hashalem*, page 240. Another reason given for reading Ruth on Shavuot is based on the Talmudic legend (Yer., *Beitsah* 2.4, 61c, and Midrash *Ruth Rabbah* 3.2) that David, Ruth's great-grandson, died on Shavuot.

[177] Midrash *Deuteronomy Rabbah* 7.3; *Song of Songs Rabbah* 1.3.

[178] See above, "Yom Kippur," C-10, page 54.

SUKKOT

[179] In the Torah (Exodus 23:16, 34:22) Sukkot is called *Chag Ha-asif*, the Festival of Ingathering. It was so important in Biblical times that it was also called *Hechag, The* Festival (I Kings 8:2).

[180] "On the eighth day you shall observe a sacred occasion. . . . It is a solemn gathering: you shall not work at your occupations" (Leviticus 23:36). The Talmud (B., *Sukkah* 47b–48a) also designates Atseret/Simchat Torah as a separate festival, e.g., one no longer celebrates in the *Sukkah* or takes up the *Lulav* and *Etrog*. In addition, the *Kiddush* for Atseret/Simchat Torah night specifically mentions the name of the festival

(*"Shemini chag ha-atseret hazeh"*), indicating it has its own special *mitzvot* as do Sukkot, Pesach, and Shavuot.

[181] In Leviticus 23:40 and Deuteronomy 16:14, the Torah designates rejoicing as one of the characteristic *mitzvot* of Sukkot.

[182] See below, D-5, page 82.

[183] See above, "Shabbat," A-11, page 25.

[184] The *Sukkah* is a temporary structure which is open to the sky. It has four walls and is covered with cut branches and plants. This covering is called the *sechach*. The *sechach* must be loosely arranged so as to allow the sky to be seen. The *Sukkah* is usually decorated with fruits and vegetables of the harvest. According to the Talmud (B., *Shabbat* 133b), we should strive to make the *Sukkah* as beautiful as possible. The enjoyment of the *mitzvah* is enhanced when we pay attention to the aesthetic dimensions of a *mitzvah* (see *"Hidur Mitzvah*: The Aesthetics of *Mitzvot*," pages 162–164).

The basic regulations for the construction of a *Sukkah* are discussed in the Mishnah (*Sukkah* 1.1–2.4) and elaborated in the codes (*Yad, Hilchot Sukkah* 4–5, and *Shulchan Aruch, Orach Chayim* 625ff). *The First Jewish Catalog* (Philadelphia: Jewish Publication Society, 1973, pages 129–130) contains simple and clear instructions for building a *Sukkah*. A number of synagogues and Jewish bookstores also sell prefabricated *Sukkot*.

[185] When the *Lulav* and *Etrog* are taken up, they are held together with the *Lulav* in the right hand and the *Etrog* in the left hand (Talmud B., *Sukkah* 37b).

It is customary, while the blessing is being recited, to hold the *Etrog* with its stem facing downward, and after the blessing, when it is waved, to hold it with stem facing upward as it grows (*Shulchan Aruch, Orach Chayim* 651.8).

[186] "R. Jochanan explained: [One waves them] to and fro [in honor of] God to whom the four directions belong, and up and down [in honor of] God to whom are heaven and earth" (Talmud B., *Sukkah* 37b).

[187] "The product of the *Hadar* tree" is the *Etrog* (Talmud B., *Sukkah* 35a) and "the boughs of leafy trees" are the myrtle (*ibid.*, 32b).

[188] Mishnah, *Sukkah* 3.4, 8; Talmud B., *Sukkah* 37b.

[189] The palm, myrtle, and willow should be fresh and green. It is customary to take special care in selecting the *Etrog*. It should be yellow with no discoloration on its skin. The tip (*Pitmah*) should not be broken.

[190] See above, "Shabbat," A-10, page 24.

[191] See above, "Pesach," note 165, page 131.

[192] The seventh day of Sukkot is known as *Hoshanah Rabbah*. Reform congregations take no special note of the day, treating it like all the other intermediate days. However, since the Middle Ages, the day has been known in the tradition as *Yom Kippur Hakatan*, a small Yom Kippur, and is seen as an opportunity for those who have not completed their repentance to do so. In addition, special clusters of willows, known as *Hoshanot*, are beaten against the ground.

[193] See note 180 above.

[194] Simchat Torah in its present form developed in the post-Talmudic period. In the Talmud (B., *Megilah* 31a), we learn that the end of Deuteronomy was assigned as the Torah reading for the second day of Shemini Atseret. Gradually, as the annual Torah-reading cycle which was dominant in the Babylonian Jewish community replaced the earlier Palestinian triennial cycle, the second day of Shemini Atseret became a joyous celebration of the completion of the Torah-reading cycle (*Siyum HaTorah*). Later, the reading from the first chapter of Genesis was added.

[195] See above, "Yom Kippur," note 125, page 125.

[196] Some Reform congregations hold Consecration on the Shabbat during Sukkot rather than on Atseret/Simchat Torah. Consecration probably developed from the custom of calling all the children to the Torah on Atseret/Simchat Torah, which is based on Deuteronomy 31:12. Moses is commanded to gather the people on Sukkot during the Sabbatical year to hear the reading of the Torah. The verse reads: "Gather the people—men, women, children and strangers in your communities—that they may hear and so learn to revere the Lord your God and to observe faithfully every word of this Torah." (See Solomon B. Freehof, *Reform Jewish Practice* I [New York: UAHC, 1964], pages 26–27).

CHANUKAH

[197] I Maccabees 4.59. The Books of Maccabees are part of an extra canonical collection called the Apocrypha. They are found only in Protestant and Catholic Bibles, but not in the Hebrew Bible.

[198] Talmud B., *Shabbat* 21b.

[199] *Ibid*. Part of the celebration of Chanukah was to display the *Menorah* so that it could be seen from outside the house (see below, A-3, page 92).

[200] Zechariah 4:1–7 is the *Haftarah* for the first Shabbat during Chanukah.

[201] Talmud, *ibid*. *Shiv-ah* is *not* suspended during Chanukah, but tradition suggested that the formal eulogy be omitted at funerals.

[202] Although Chanukah is not a Biblical festival, the Rabbis required that blessings be recited over the lighting of Chanukah lights and used the same formula as is used for Biblical *mitzvot*—"Blessed is the Lord our God, Ruler of the Universe, by Whose *mitzvot* we are hallowed, Who commands us . . ." (Talmud B., *Sukkah* 46a).

[203] In *Soferim* 20.6 it is stated that we are only permitted to look at the Chanukah candles but not use them, as they are exclusively a symbol of thanksgiving for the miracle of deliverance which Chanukah commemorates.

[204] Since the lighting of Shabbat candles ushers in Shabbat (see above "Shabbat," A-12, page 25), and because of the traditional prohibition against lighting a fire on Shabbat, the Chanukah candles are lit before Shabbat candles. For the same reason, the Chanukah candles are lit after *Havdalah* on Saturday night.

[205] Talmud B., *Shabbat* 24a

[206] The eating of dairy dishes is associated with the story of Judith who slew the Assyrian leader, Holofernes, after he laid siege to the town of Bethulea near Jerusalem. It is reported that Judith prepared a meal of wine and cheese and brought it to Holofernes's tent. When the general had fallen into a drunken stupor, Judith killed him. Eventually this story was joined to the lore of the bravery of the Hasmoneans. Dishes cooked in oil are associated with the story of the cruse of oil, which

according to the Talmudic legend lasted eight days (see *Rama* on *Orach Chayim* 670.2).

[207] Legend tells that during the time of the Hellenistic and Roman persecution, when the study of Torah was forbidden by the ruling powers, students used the game of Dreidel as a subterfuge to hide their studying. *Dreidel* is a Yiddish word from *drehn*, to spin; *Sevivon* is its Hebrew equivalent.

[208] In Israel, the letter פ, *Pe*, is substituted for the letter ש, *Shin*, rendering the meaning of the four letters, *Nes Gadol Haya Po*, "A great miracle happened here" (i.e., in Jerusalem).

PURIM

[209] The fifteenth of Adar is known as *Shushan Purim*, because according to the Book of Esther (9:18), the Jews of Shushan (the capital) celebrated Purim on the fifteenth of Adar rather than on the fourteenth. The Mishnah (*Megilah* 1.1) therefore ordained that cities which were surrounded by walls since the time of Joshua should observe Purim on the fifteenth. Jerusalem is considered to be one such city, and thus the Jews of Jerusalem observe Purim on the fifteenth.

The Shabbat preceding Purim is called *Shabbat Zachor* (Sabbath of Remembrance), because the additional Torah reading for that Shabbat (Deuteronomy 25:17–19) begins with the words "*Zachor et asher asa lecha Amalek*," "Remember what Amalek did to you." In Jewish tradition Amalek is identified with Haman, the villain of the Purim story. *Shabbat Zachor* serves as preparation for Purim.

[210] While this is the popular understanding of the meaning of Purim, the original meaning of the Book of Esther (which became overshadowed by later history) was to tell the story of two assimilated Jews who tried to make it as Gentiles but could not. This understanding of the story remains relevant for Jews today. Assimilation did not protect the Jews of Europe from becoming victims of the *Sho-ah*. Judaism, the Jewish people, and the world are better served by Jews who proudly acknowledge their heritage and actively oppose anti-Semites. The story further emphasizes the tragic necessity of Jews to defend themselves against those who would kill them.

211 The Jews of Jerusalem observe Purim on the fifteenth of Adar. See note
209 above.

212 The Talmud (B., *Megilah* 4a) prescribes the reading of *Megilat Ester* at
both the evening and morning services.

213 *Shulchan Aruch, Orach Chayim* 690.18.

214 Esther 9:22 designates Purim as "days of festive joy, feasting, and merrymaking." The mood on Purim is so joyous that the Talmud (B.
Megilah 7b) is permissive concerning the drinking of intoxicants on
Purim: "As Rava said, 'A person should be so merry [with drink] on
Purim that he does not know the difference between 'cursed be Haman'
and 'blessed is Mordecai.' " On no other occasion is such conduct
encouraged.
  While we are not encouraging intoxication, it should be clear that
the atmosphere on Purim is unlike that of any other holiday. The
celebration is unrestrained, with laughter and merrymaking the order
of the day.

215 The wearing of costumes, especially of the characters in the Purim story,
is part of the celebration. Purim is the one occasion when men and
women are permitted to wear each others' clothes (*Rama* on *Orach
Chayim* 696.8). In Israel, Purim is celebrated with costume parades,
floats, and bands called *Adlayada*, which is based on the Talmudic
phrase "*Ad dela yada bein arur Haman levaruch Mordechai*," i.e., "A
person should be so merry on Purim that he does not know the difference between 'cursed is Haman' and 'blessed is Mordecai' " (Talmud
B., *Megilah* 7b).

216 Esther 9:22.

217 *Ibid.* Gifts to the poor at this season are particularly significant, because
they recognize that the survival of Jews is in part dependent upon
other Jews expressing care and concern.
  The giving of *Tzedakah* on Purim can also be linked to the ancient
half-*Shekel* tax paid to support the Temple (Exodus 30:12). The Rabbis
ordained that the Shabbat immediately preceding the first of Adar
contain a warning that the tax was coming due (Mishnah, *Shekalim*
1.1). Therefore Exodus 30:11–16 is read in addition to the weekly
portion. The Shabbat is known as *Shabbat Shekalim*.

ROSH CHODESH

[218] See, for example: I Samuel 20; II Kings 4:23; Isaiah 1:13; Amos 8:5; Psalms 81:4; and Ezra 45:17.

[219] Mishnah, *Rosh Hashanah* 2.5–7.

[220] While Reform Jews consider the first day of each month as Rosh Chodesh, traditional observance also includes the thirtieth day of the preceding month, where the preceding month has 30 days (as opposed to 29). Thus, in other congregations Rosh Chodesh will be observed either one or two days, depending on the length of the preceding month.

[221] Talmud Yer., *Ta-anit* 1.6; *Tosafot, Rosh Hashanah* 23a, *s.v. "Mishum bitul melacha la-am shenei yamim"; Aruch Hashulchan, Orach Chayim* 417.10.

[222] Targum Jonathan to Exodus 32:3.

[223] The connection between women and Rosh Chodesh probably has its origin in the parallel between the lunar cycle and the female menstrual cycle.

YOM HA-ATSMAUT

[224] *CCAR Yearbook*, vol. 80, 1970, page 39; see also *ibid.*, 1969, page 143.

YOM HASHO-AH

[225] *CCAR Yearbook*, vol. 87, 1977, page 87.

TISH-AH BE-AV

[226] In the Mishnah (*Ta-anit* 4.6), a number of tragic events are said to have happened on the 9th of Av: "It was decreed against our ancestors that they should not enter the Land of Israel, the Temple was destroyed

the first and second time, and Bethar was captured, and the city [Jerusalem] was ploughed up."

[227] For example: In 1290 King Edward I signed the edict expelling the Jews from England; in 1914, Archduke Ferdinand of Austria was shot on the eve of Tish-ah Be-Av, leading to the mobilization for World War I on the next day.

OTHERS

[228] Mishnah, *Rosh Hashanah* 1.1. "*Tu*" is the number 15 written in Hebrew letters. Each alphabet letter in Hebrew is also a number. *Tet*, ט, equals nine; *vav*, ו, equals six. When they are written together, ט״ו, they may be pronounced "*tu*."

[229] An old Kabbalistic text, *Sefer Peri Ets Hadar*, attributed to Hayim Vital, contains a fully written version of the *Seder*. Some Reform congregations have revived this old tradition, and a number of rabbis have produced their own texts for the *Seder*.

[230] The prophet Zechariah (8:19) mentions four fasts: the fast of the fourth month, the fast of the fifth month, the fast of the seventh month, and the fast of the tenth month, which the Talmud B. (*Rosh Hashanah*) identifies as follows: the fast of the fourth month refers to the seventeenth of Tamuz; the fast of the fifth month refers to Tish-ah Be-Av (the ninth of Av); the fast of the seventh month refers to the Fast of Gedaliah; and the fast of the tenth month refers to the tenth of Tevet.

[231] The day before Purim, the thirteenth of Adar, is called *Ta-anit Ester*, the fast of Esther. It is most likely based on the fast which Esther asked Mordecai to proclaim after he informed her of Haman's plot to destroy the Jews (Esther 4:16).

[232] "Five tragedies befell our ancestors on the seventeenth of Tamuz. . . . On the seventeenth of Tamuz the Ten Commandments were smashed, the Daily Whole Offering ceased, the City of Jerusalem was breached, and Apostomus burnt the Torah and an idol was set up in the Temple" (Mishnah, *Ta-anit* 4.6).

[233] The tenth of Tevet signals the beginning of the Siege of Jerusalem by

the Babylonian King Nebuchadnezzar (Talmud B., *Rosh Hashanah* 16b).

[234] The Fast of Gedaliah occurs on the third of Tishri and commemorates the murder of Gedaliah ben Ahikam who was appointed governor of Judah by Nebuchadnezzar after the first destruction of Jerusalem (586 B.C.E.). The incident is recorded in Jeremiah 40:7–41:3 and II Kings 24:22–26.

Appendix

BRIEF ESSAYS

SHABBAT AS PROTEST*

W. GUNTHER PLAUT

IF Shabbat is to have significance, it must confront one of modern civilization's greatest curses, its internal and external unrest. This unrest arises from the twin facts that the life we lead is frequently without goals and that we are involved in competition without end.

I view Shabbat as potentially an enormous relief from and protest against the basic causes of unrest. Once a week it provides us with an opportunity to address ourselves to the meaning of human existence rather than the struggle for survival; to persons rather than things; to Creation and our part in it; to society and its needs; to ourselves as individuals and yet as social beings. This has been called "the inner source of leisure," the setting of goals which are both realistic and within one's reach, yet also beyond one's self.

There are few better places for such redirection than a religious service, whose major function ought to be not just the repetition of well-worn formulae but the celebration of human goals. If nothing happens to us during this or any Shabbat experience except an enlarging of our vision, we will have gained a new perspective of life's meaning and will have diminished our sense of unrest. That will be Shabbat rest in the sense required by our time.

Endless competition is a specific form of restlessness. Shabbat can be a surcease from and a protest against all forms of competition even when they come in attractive packages marked "self-advancement" or "self-improvement." Shabbat in this sense may be viewed as a "useless" day. Our ancestors had a keen understanding of the fact that sleep on Shabbat was a form of coming closer to God. We must once again understand that doing nothing, being silent and open to the world, letting things happen

*Condensed from "The Sabbath as Protest—Thoughts on Work and Leisure in the Automated Society," by W. Gunther Plaut, in *Tradition and Change in the Jewish Experience*, ed. A. Leland Jamison (Syracuse: Syracuse University Press, 1978), pages 169–183.

inside, can be as important as, and sometimes more important than what we commonly call useful.

Formerly a person who did not work was considered useless; what we need now is a purposeful uselessness, an activity (or non-activity!) which is important in that it becomes an essential protest against that basic unrest which comes from competition without end.

In the Jewish context it may therefore be suggested that on Shabbat one abstains from everything which on one level or another may be considered usefully competitive. Shabbat gives us a quantity of free time and thereby a quality potential of freedom-time, when a person can search for the self and in some area do for self and others what in the work-a-day one cannot.

It has been said that there are four states of human consciousness: imaginative, active, reflexive, and contemplative. The two middle states (activity and reflexive response) characterize our automated society; the other two (imagination and contemplation) are the redeeming features which make life livable. These are the qualities to which Shabbat addresses itself, for imagination is a form of freedom and contemplation is rest from unrest.

◆ ◆

FASTING ON YOM KIPPUR

YOM Kippur is a day set apart by the Torah for us to "practice self-denial" (Leviticus 23:27). The "self-denial" which seems to be most expressive of Yom Kippur is fasting, abstaining from food and drink for the entire day.

Fasting is an opportunity for each of us to observe Yom Kippur in a most personal way. It is a day of intense self-searching and earnest communication with the Almighty. This search requires an internal calm which derives from slowing down our biological rhythm. Fasting on Yom Kippur provides the key to our inner awakening.

On Yom Kippur we seek reconciliation with God and humanity. Repentance (*Teshuvah*) involves a critical self-assessment of the past year and the resolve to avoid lapses in sensitivity in the future. *Teshuvah* requires discipline. Our fasting on Yom Kippur demonstrates our willingness to submit to discipline. How can we atone for our excesses toward others unless we can curb appetites which depend on no one but ourselves? To set boundaries for our own conduct in this very private matter is to begin the path toward controlling our public behavior.

The fast of Yom Kippur reaches beyond our inner spiritual awakening and discipline into our ethical behavior. In the *Haftarah* we read on Yom Kippur morning of the prophet Isaiah providing us with the ultimate goal of our fast—to unlock the shackles of injustice, to undo the fetters of bondage, to let the oppressed go free, to share bread with the hungry (Isaiah 58:1–14).

Finally, to fast on the Day of Atonement is an act of solidarity with the suffering of the Jewish people. Through fasting we are drawn closer to all who live lives of deprivation. Our faith demands more of us than twenty-four hours of abstinence from food. It demands that upon the completion of our fast we will turn back to the world prepared to act with love and compassion. In this way fasting touches the biological as well as the spiritual aspects of our being.

◆ ◆

FRAGMENTS OF FAITH: ON HOLY DAY LITURGY

HARVEY J. FIELDS

THE celebration of Jewish holidays provides some intriguing insights into the nature of Jewish thought and spirituality. Each holy day is different; each has its own focus and its own special cluster of meanings. The study of selected holy day prayers helps one understand the crucial themes and values that take the Jew from one year to the next.

Yamim Nora-im—Days of Awe

The Torah proclaims that on the first day of the seventh month (Tishri) a sacred occasion shall be celebrated with "loud blasts," and ten days later Yom Kippur (Day of Atonement) should be observed with "self-denial" and expiation before the Lord."[1] Through centuries of commemoration the

[1]Leviticus 23:23–32.

sacred season has evolved into a time for self-scrutiny and *Teshuvah* (reconciliation with God).

The liturgy of the *Selichot* service, just before Rosh Hashanah, is an overture introducing the music and themes of the sacred season. The service is based on the *Vidui* (confessional) prayers that are at the heart of the Yom Kippur liturgy. We begin to probe our failings and weaknesses calling upon "*El Melech, yoshev al kise rachamim*," Sovereign God, enthroned in mercy. The liturgy then leads us to the Thirteen Attributes of God's compassion, first ennunciated by Moses.[2] The congregation prays "*Shema Kolenu*" (Hear our voice) and recites the "*Ashamnu*" (We have all committed offenses) and "*Al chet schechatanu lefanecha*" (For the sin we have committed against You). Of equal importance to the text of these prayers is their musical setting, creating a mood which opens us to the sacred possibilities of Rosh Hashanah and Yom Kippur. The *Selichot* service concludes with a long blast of the *Shofar*.

The *Tefilah* (or *Amidah*) of both Rosh Hashanah and Yom Kippur, takes the form of the seven sections familiar in the Shabbat and festival liturgies. For the *Yamim Nora-im*, however, there are special interpolations. Into the very first paragraph, the *Avot*, in which we introduce ourselves, as it were, to God, writers during the Gaonic period fused the notion of God's love for our ancestors Abraham, Isaac, and Jacob with the petitions "Remember us unto life" and "Inscribe us in the Book of Life." The petition is repeated within the "*Sim Shalom*" (prayer for peace) which comes at the end of the *Tefilah*. Both of these additions emphasize the central purpose of the *Yamim Nora-im* as a sacred time for rectifying behavior and renewing one's relationship with that source of mercy that sustains life and makes repentance possible.

Human weakness and the uncertainty of human existence form the emotional ground for the "*Unetaneh Tokef*" prayer, which contains a vivid description of heavenly judgment. Each life is counted. All deeds are sifted. The destiny of each human being is recorded on Rosh Hashanah, yet it remains unsealed until Yom Kippur. During the Ten Days of Repentance turning and transformation are possible. The "*Unetaneh Tokef*" declares that it is within human power to "temper judgment's severe decree" through repentance, prayer, and charity.

[2]Exodus 34:6–7.

The motif of God's love culminating in the human response of repentance flows throughout the original forty-five invocations of the "*Avinu, Malkenu.*" Within *Gates of Repentance* various versions are offered, all concluding with the longing, "*Avinu, Malkenu* . . . treat us generously and with kindness, and be our help."

At the heart of the Rosh Hashanah worship is the *Shofar* service. The *Shofar* is blown on Rosh Hashanah morning, following the Torah reading. The Talmudic sages defined and prescribed the three musical phrases— *Teki-ah, Teru-ah,* and *Shevarim.* Rabbi Akiba first linked the *Shofar* sounds to the three themes of *Malchuyot* (Kingship), *Zichronot* (Remembrance), and *Shofarot* (*Shofar* sounds).[3]

The *Shofar* service themes are carefully constructed around Biblical verses drawn from the Torah, Prophets, and Writings. They celebrate the mystery and majesty of God's power. The familiar "*Aleinu,*" originally placed here in the liturgy and then adopted as a standard concluding feature of daily and holiday worship, announces God's Kingship (*Malchuyot*) and the hope that God's rule will transform and perfect the world. In the section called *Zichronot,* God's awesome remembering is described. Nothing from Genesis to the thoughts of each human being is lost: "You unravel every mystery . . . You remember every deed." And so the congregation prays: "Remember Your love for us, the covenant You made with Abraham on Mount Moriah." If all is remembered then the covenant endures, and there is hope for a future where love and compassion will triumph. That Messianic aspiration constitutes the sense of optimism overflowing in the *Shofarot* section. The *Shofar* sounds recall the moments of revelation at Sinai and anticipate that all the yearnings released there will ultimately lead to the time when "the great *Shofar* will announce our freedom" and "bring lasting joy to Zion and to Jerusalem."

For many Jews, Yom Kippur evening is known as "*Kol Nidrei* Eve." It is the haunting melody and the cluster of associations around an ancient formula of words that draws so many to that Holy Day service. Actually, the Hebrew-Aramaic text, which has its origins in the Talmud,[4] passed through several battles and transformations. Seeing in it the intention of annulling promises (vows) made "from this Day of Atonement till the

[3]Talmud B., *Rosh Hashanah* 34a (also 16a).
[4]Mishnah, *Nedarim* 3.1; Talmud B., *Nedarim* 23b.

next," many efforts to expunge the formula from the liturgy were made.[5] Most were unsuccessful. "*Kol Nidrei*" persists, perhaps, because it reveals us as the fallible creatures that we are and exposes our great need for forgiveness. On Yom Kippur we realize that we are frail creatures, embodiments of clashing needs and ambitions, and that while we may piously promise to live out our highest values, we know that we may fail or be bent to compromise. "*Kol Nidrei*" appeals to us because it is a formula based on the belief in God, something that struggling human beings require from one Yom Kippur to the next.

The *Vidui* (Confession of Sin) is repeated at each Yom Kippur service. Borrowing from the humble meditations of Rabbi Hamnuna and Rav,[6] the formula includes the admission, "We are not so arrogant and stiff-necked as to say before You . . . we are perfect and have not sinned." (Note the plural, indicating our responsibility for all Jews.) Both the "*Ashamnu*" and "*Al Chet*" prayers were also written during the Gaonic period and are arranged in alphabetical order, as if to indicate that on Yom Kippur we are to grapple with all our sins from *Alef* to *Tav*. Within traditional texts, the "*Al Chet*" contains forty-four lines, a double alphabet of confessions, matching the same number of lines found within the "*Avinu Malkenu*." The sins detailed do not mention ritual matters; they deal with ethical transgressions.

After the Temple's destruction (70 C.E.), poets continued to recall with awe every aspect of the sacred service: the priest's dress, his confession, his entrance into the Holy of Holies chamber, and the awesome pronouncement of God's name. Memories of the ancient Temple service were preserved in the *Avodah* section of the traditional morning service. Within Reform Judaism the recollections have been shifted to the afternoon service, and expanded into an examination and celebration of the people of Israel's relationship to God. The Jerusalem Temple service is recalled, but it is placed within the context of all the triumphs and tragedies a Jew carries into his/her confrontation with God.[7]

Yom Kippur concludes with *Ne-ilah* (Closing Service). In it the prayer

---

[5]Rabbi Amram Gaon labelled *Kol Nidrei* "*minhag shetut*" (foolish custom); others also opposed it. See Jacob Mann, *Texts and Studies* (Philadelphia: 1935).
[6]Talmud B., *Yoma* 87b.
[7]*Gates of Repentance*, pages 420–425.

]

"Inscribe us in the Book of Life" is altered to "Seal us in the Book of Life."
Ne-ilah culminates the great day of soul-searching, fasting, and atonement.
In place of the "*Al Chet*," the *Vidui* section emphasizes our human uniqueness ("Yet from the beginning You set us apart to stand erect before You"),
and expresses the hope that "turning away from violence and oppression,
we may turn back to You and do Your will with a perfect heart."[8] At sunset
the fast comes to an end with a reminder of the sacred partnership between
the human and Divine, and with a long *Shofar* blast filled with yearnings
for a new year of favor and mercy.

The Pilgrimage Festivals

The distinctive prayers of the Festivals, in the *Tefilah* (or *Amidah*), were
first formulated in the Talmud and then recast during the Gaonic period
in Babylonia. The central benediction of the *Tefilah* opens with the declaration, "*Ata vechartanu*" (In love and favor, O God, You have chosen us
from all the peoples ... .). Reference is made to each of the Festivals as
times of joy and seasons for celebrating the sacred obligations that bind
Jews to God's service.

The next paragraph is known as the "*Ya-aleh veyayo.*" It is built on a
fragment of faith which holds that just as Jews recall and commemorate
the Festival, so will God remember them for goodness, blessing, and fullness
of life. The whole section concludes with words of praise for God who
confers sacred distinction upon (the Sabbath), Israel, and the Festivals.

Another unique feature of the Festival liturgy is the *Hallel* (Psalms
113–118). The psalms were originally sung at the Temple ritual, and then
were included in synagogue services for the Festivals. A shorter *Hallel*
(omitting verses from Psalms 115 and 116) was created by Babylonian
Jews especially for the last six days of Pesach and for the New Moon
commemoration.[9] Israel Abrahams once commented that "The Hallel,
sounding the whole gamut of trust and despair, dejection and triumph,

---

[8]See *Yoma* 87b; also comments by Max Arzt, *Justice and Mercy: Commentary on
Liturgy of the New Year and the Day of Atonement* (New York: Holt, Rinehart and
Winston, 1963), pages 277–281.
[9]See J. H. Hertz, *Daily Prayer Book* (New York: Bloch Publishing Co., 1955),
page 757.

agony and release, with praise running through the whole, retells to Israel the story of his chequered national life."[10]

The *Yizkor* service, originally composed for Yom Kippur, may be traced to the Gaonic period in Babylonia, yet it did not become a permanent part of Jewish worship until after the Crusades. The pogroms and massacres left Jews traumatized and with a need to express their communal sorrow. Later, *Yizkor* services were also added to Festival worship. *Yizkor* provides moments for recalling loved ones, for sensing the devotion of those who have handed the Torah tradition from one generation to the next, and for facing the Psalmist's lesson, "So teach us to number our days that we may grow wise in heart."

Chanukah and Purim

The liturgy of Chanukah and Purim include the recitation of the "*Al hanisim*" (redeeming wonders) prayer. Written sometime during the 7th century in Babylonia, "*Al hanisim*" was included by Rabbi Amram Gaon in his first *Siddur* and added to the *Hoda-ah* (Thanksgiving) section of the *Tefilah*. For each of the holidays, special mention is made of the historic redemption of the people from their oppressors. Amram's original version included the petition, "Just as You did [redeeming wonders] with them, accomplish wonders and miracles on our behalf at this time. . . . " Here Chanukah and Purim articulate the aspirations of a persecuted people. The "*Al hanisim*" prayer provides a playback of memories about the Hasmoneans (for Chanukah) and about Mordecai and Esther (Purim), and is meant to inspire Jewish pride and hope.[11]

Conclusion

When the Talmudic sage, Rabbi Eliezer, fell ill and his disciples visited him, they asked: "Master, teach us the paths of life so that we may through them win the life of the future world." He told them, in part: "When you

[10]See *Sifrei* to Deuteronomy 21:1–9, and *Tanchuma, Ha-azinu*. Note also references in A. Z. Idelsohn, *Jewish Liturgy and its Development* (New York: Henry Holt and Company, 1932), pages 230–232; and Psalms 90:12.
[11]*Gates of Prayer*, pages 68–69.

pray know before whom you are standing."[12] In prayer a Jew experiences God as awesome Creator, as mysterious Giver of Torah, and as that wondrous Power of Redemption at work in history. The holy day liturgy provides a Jew with prose and poetry, fragments of faith from ages past, with which we may today stand before God.

◆ ◆

YIZKOR

ONE of the most moving portions of the Yom Kippur and Festival worship services is the Memorial Service (*Hazkarat Neshamot*).* Popularly known as *Yizkor* after the opening words of the silent devotion "*Yizkor Elohim*" ("May God remember [the soul of]. . ."), it emphasizes the transience of life, out yearning for eternity, and the inspiration provided by the memory of the deceased. The service reminds us that time moves swiftly forward and bids us, "number our days that we may grow wise in heart" (Psalm 90:12).

Memory is a precious gift, for it transforms the discrete moments of our lives and events in history into an unfolding narrative. We become acutely aware of being a part of an eternal people that began a spiritual journey in the distant past with its goal to be realized in the remote future. Through the words and music of the service we become conscious not only of our own mortality but also of the sacred opportunity that we have in our brief lives to perform acts of sanctification which may improve our lot and the lot of humanity generally.

The life of the Jewish people is composed of sacred moments which, when recalled, inspire us to live our lives according to certain Judaic values. For example, the bitter experience of slavery is tasted in the eating of *Maror* on Pesach. By recreating the sense of physical and spiritual bondage we commit ourselves to an ethical system which teaches us that freedom is

---

[12]Talmud B., *Berachot* 28b.

Yizkor is recited in all Reform congregations on Yom Kippur and on the seventh day of Pesach, and in many congregations on Shavuot and Atseret/Simchat Torah as well.

essential for human development. How we act toward others must be judged in the light of the verse, "We were slaves to Pharaoh in Egypt" (Deuteronomy 6:21).

On Shavuot, when we hear the Ten Commandments read, we are transported backward to Mt. Sinai and utter in our hearts the ancient formula of commitment *Na-aseh Venishma*, "We will diligently hearken" (Exodus 24:7). The ancient covenant is renewed through memory. By observing the *mitzvot* of Shavuot our individual memory becomes part of the collective memory of the Jewish people.

For Jews, the inspiring figures in both the remote and recent past remain as constant companions and role models. They teach by precept and example. Their story is our story. Their courage, wisdom, and goodness are a permanent challenge.

Memory roots us firmly in the past. The fertile soil of more than four thousand years of history nurtures us, providing us with a clear sense of who we are. Our lives add new branches to the tree of the Jewish people. A living past provides for a meaningful present and hope for the future.

As we recite the *Yizkor* prayer we mention in our hearts the names of all who were close to us—grandparents, parents, friends, and relatives. By preserving the memory of those who were our teachers we are encouraged to continue the tasks they bequeathed to us. The memorial service is an act of faith that goodness does not die with a person but exists in the memory of those who remain alive.

Our thoughts also turn to those of our people who sought, through their lives and through their deaths, to testify to the undying spirit of the Jewish people and its mission as a holy nation.

In the past custom dictated that only those whose parents were deceased attended the Memorial Service. But recognizing that so many who died in the *Sho-ah* have no one to recite *Kaddish* for them, and realizing that memory helps to forge a chain of solidarity and continuity between our generation and the past, all are encouraged to participate.

The words of the memorial prayer *El Malei Rachamim* ("O God full of compassion") is a petition for the repose of the deceased and an expression of our faith in the ultimate sacredness of humankind.

Death removes our loved ones from their earthly abode, yet Jewish tradition affirms the faith that the divine spark in every human soul has a permanent dwelling place with the Eternal. The mystery of what lies beyond the grave is shrouded by an impenetrable veil, yet within our hearts is planted the hope for eternity. Memory is the sacred link between past and future and between time and eternity.

Immortality is a word which we can associate only with God, but the blessing of memory and the blessedness of the memory of the righteous can be guaranteed by our devoted recall. The *mitzvah* of *Yizkor* is a door that opens on eternity, making the present more significant by allowing us to combine memory and hope.

♦ ♦

TORAH AND *HAFTARAH* READINGS

ONE of the most dramatic moments of the synagogue service occurs when the Torah scrolls are removed from the Ark and read before the congregation. Since the period of the Babylonian exile the public reading of the Torah has been central to Jewish worship. The special readings from the Torah and Prophets on the High Holy Days and Festivals link us to an ancient tradition. The public reading of the Torah on a festival is first mentioned in the *Tanach* itself (Nehemiah 8), and was clearly a fixed procedure by the third century of the common era, when the Mishnah was compiled.[1]

The selection of readings for the Festival and High Holy Day cycle reveals yet another aspect of the profound influence of the early Rabbis on the development of Judaism. They chose passages appropriate to each festival which would give the essential message of the holy day. Even as they created new observances for the festivals to allow for a Jewish religious faith no longer linked to the Biblical sacrificial system, they also provided lessons from both the Torah and Prophets which would address the ongoing significance of each festival.

Torah study, *Talmud Torah*, is an organic part of our Jewish observance (see *Gates of Mitzvah*, page 19, E-1; page 22, F-1; page 39, E-5). Just as

---

[1]The Mishnah (*Megilah* 3.4–6) details the readings for special Sabbaths and for the Festivals and makes it clear that the Torah was also read on every Monday, Thursday, and Shabbat afternoon.

reviewing the weekly Torah portion each week is preparation for Shabbat, so the study of the special scriptural readings for the festivals is part of the preparation for the festivals. In the sections that follow, the central themes of each reading are highlighted, and the relationship between the Biblical reading and the festival clarified.[2]

The High Holydays

On Rosh Hashanah morning, as we celebrate the New Year as *Yom Hazikaron*, a day of memorial, and contemplate this central theme in the prayer "*Zochrenu lechayim*" ("Remember us unto life"), we are jarred by the challenging narrative of Abraham's binding of Isaac (Genesis 22:1–19). Tradition refers to this passage as a remembrance of hope for life, even in despair, and as a testimony to Abraham's devotion. A further link is established between the ram caught in the thicket by its horns, which served as a substitute sacrifice for Isaac, and the *Shofar* (ram's horn) which is sounded immediately following the Torah service. The portions from the prophetic books are either selections from Samuel's call to God's service (I Samuel 1) or selected verses from Nehemiah 8, where Rosh Hashanah is commemorated by the public reading of the Torah.

The Creation narrative (Genesis 1:2–3) serves as an alternate Torah reading. Talmudic tradition designates the first of Tishri as the day on which the world was created and the liturgy reminds us that "this is the day the world was brought into being."[3] The prophetic readings from Isaiah 55:6–13 or Jeremiah 31:1–19 are both messages of hope for the restoration of Israel to its land. So, as we celebrate the creation of the cosmos on Rosh Hashanah, we pray for the recreation of the people of Israel in peace and harmony.

Personal resolve to do *Teshuvah* and the affirmation of human beings as moral free agents form the central theme of the Torah reading on Yom

---

[2]In keeping with a tradition that indicates great variation of selection for the synagogue readings, rabbis of the Central Conference of American Rabbis have from time to time revised the Scriptural reading for Reform congregations. The most recent list was compiled by A. Stanley Dreyfus in *Gates of the House*, pages 283–296 and *Gates of Repentance*, pages 124–135, 193–203, 342–349, and 452–463. For a list of readings in Orthodox and Conservative synagogues one should consult a traditional *Machzor*, or festival prayerbook.

[3]Talmud B., *Rosh Hashanah* 11a.

Kippur morning. The verses from the Book of Deuteronomy (29:9–14; 30:11–20) emphasize that we choose life in order that we might live— thus, we elevate life above a biological function into an ever-growing series of conscious choices to improve our lot and the lot of all humanity. The prophetic reading from Isaiah (58:1–14) complements the theme of choice. Isaiah's admonition reminds us that ritual behavior which condones oppression and economic irresponsibility is an unacceptable life choice.

The ethical and ritual demands of holiness are enumerated in the afternoon reading from the Book of Leviticus (19:1–4, 9–18, 32–37) which calls upon us to be holy, for the Lord our God is holy. Holiness is not expressed in ritual purity but in a series of demands for proper conduct. The prophetic reading for Yom Kippur afternoon is taken from the Book of Jonah. The prophet wrestles with the Divine demand that he preach to the people of Nineveh so that God might not destroy the city. Jonah's spiritual odyssey represents the conflict between our urge toward higher ethical demands and our desire to escape from the awesome task which is present in all who set forth on the challenging journey to make holiness the goal of life.

The Three Pilgrimage Festivals

The readings for Pesach commence with the narration from the Book of Exodus (12:37–42; 13:3–10) describing the departure from Egypt, the injunction to observe the Festival by eating unleavened bread, and the retelling of the marvelous deliverance of Israel. The prophetic reading comes from Isaiah (43:1–15) and emphasizes God's deliverance of Israel, while calling upon Israel to act as witnesses to God's benevolent care.

The Torah reading for the next day (Exodus 13:14–16) continues the narrative of redemption, emphasizing the obligation to tell one's children that Israel was freed through the wondrous acts of God. Each of the other intermediate days of the Festival (*Chol Hamo-ed*) has a brief reading from different books of the Torah which relate the various commandments to observe Pesach.[4]

On the intermediate Shabbat of both Pesach and Sukkot we read of God revealing himself to Moses in the cleft of the rock and the Divine

---

[4]*Gates of the House*, page 295.

commandments about the Pilgrimage Festivals (Exodus 33:12–34:46). The prophetic reading is taken from Ezekiel (37:1–14) and describes the ultimate triumph of God over the forces of evil.

This Shabbat is marked by reading the Song of Songs, the scroll appointed by the Rabbis for reading at Pesach. The lyrical passages remind us of the rebirth of nature in the spring, and the intense love between the characters in the song has been compared to the intense love between God and Israel.

The readings for Pesach conclude with the Song of the Sea (Exodus 14:30–15:21), a victory song celebrating the departure of Israel from Egypt. This reading is complemented by the poems of victory either from II Samuel (22:1–51) or from the prophet Isaiah, who speaks about the messianic triumph of God's Kingdom (Isaiah 11:1–6; 12:1–6).

Since Shavuot commemorates the giving of Torah, the Torah reading describes the preparation of the people at Sinai and the giving of the Ten Commandments (Exodus 19:1–8; 20:1–14). The prophetic portion from Isaiah (42:1–12) focuses on the implications of receiving the covenant. Israel is a "Covenant People" and "a light unto the nations." On Shavuot the Book of Ruth is read. The Rabbis saw in Ruth's acceptance of Judaism a parallel to Israel's acceptance of the covenant.

The readings for the Festival of Sukkot follow the pattern of those for Pesach wherein the injunction and explanations of the Festival are read from the Torah. On the first day, Leviticus 23:33–44, which describes the taking up of the four species and celebrating in the *Sukkot*, is read. The prophetic readings are taken either from Zechariah (14:7–9, 16–21) or Isaiah (35:1–10 or 32:1–8, 14–20). In these passages the prophet declares that Israel's ultimate deliverance will take place on Sukkot. On the intermediate days of the Festivals short selections are read from various books of the Torah which detail the various Biblical observances of Sukkot.[5] The Torah and *Haftarah* readings for the intermediate Shabbat on Sukkot are the same as on the intermediate Shabbat of Pesach (Exodus 33:12–34:46, and Ezekiel 37:1–14). Complementing these Torah and prophetic portions is the reading of the Scroll of Ecclesiastes (*Kohelet*). The commemoration of a fall festival which exemplifies the transitory nature of life and all its fragility is reflected in this book.

[5]*Ibid.*, pages 293–294.

Sukkot ends by celebrating the completion of the cycle of all Torah readings for the year. Atseret/Simchat Torah signifies both ending and beginning anew, for we conclude the last chapter of Deuteronomy (34:1–12) and immediately read thereafter the first chapter of Genesis (1:1–2:3). The prophetic reading from Joshua (1:1–18) emphasizes the theme of ending and new beginning. Moses has died and Joshua immediately assumes the mantel of leadership.

The beauty and significance of the Festivals are further opened to us by a careful reading and preparation of the Biblical passage. Each cycle of readings enables us to touch our past with all its insights, and to awaken in ourselves the possibility of a richer and more meaningful observance of the High Holy Days and the Festivals.

◆ ◆

FESTIVAL FOODS

STEVEN M. FINK

THE holiday spirit is a complicated web of feelings and expectations. The crispness of the air, the best china on the table, the cleaning of the house, and the new suit of clothes are all important elements of preparation for the festival we are about to celebrate. The delicious aroma of holiday foods transmits wonderful memories and ethnic consciousness. The honey cake just out of the oven tells us it is Rosh Hashanah; the crisp, slightly oniony smell of potato *Latkes* reminds us it is Chanukah; the making of *Matzah Balls* and *Charoset* heralds the beginning of Pesach.

Holiday foods enhance and elevate our festival celebration. By reserving certain distinctive foods for special days, each holiday meal takes on its own joyous and familiar character. Festival foods reinforce the meaning of the holiday and add to the celebratory mood of the diners. Every Jewish family has its favorite holiday foods. Through time these foods have become imbued with beautiful associations and warm memories. They have acquired a uniqueness and even a sanctity of their own which are handed down from generation to generation. These special recipes are part of our rich cultural and religious heritage.

Holiday foods are as different and varied as the Jewish people. Wherever

Jews have lived they have adopted and embellished foods from the local culture. Foods from ancient Egypt and Rome, medieval Germany and Spain, and nineteenth-century Russia and Hungary grace the holiday table. The spicy and aromatic cookery of the Sephardic Jews is as rich and diversified as that of Ashkenazic Jewry.

The traditional Sabbath eve meal often consists of chicken soup with *Kreplach* (meat filled dough), chopped liver or *Gefilte Fish*, chicken or fish prepared in any number of ways, a *Kugel* (noodle or potato pudding), and vegetables. The traditional dish for Shabbat afternoon in Eastern Europe was *Cholent* (meaning "hot"). Potatoes, *Kasha* (groats), and the little meat available were placed into a pot and cooked for twenty-four hours in the community oven before being carried home by a child for the noon meal. In this country, a typical *Cholent* includes brisket, onions, lima beans, and barley or potatoes. It is a perfect dish for crock pot cooking. Sephardic dishes for Shabbat would include various vegetables, such as carrots, zucchini, or eggplants stuffed with ground meat, or delicious rice-based dishes.

Sweet foods, symbolizing the anticipated sweetness of the year ahead, are prominent among the delicacies that constitute the Rosh Hashanah festive meal. Apples dipped in honey, *Lekach* (honey and spice cake), *Tayglach* (honey and nut pastry), and honey cake are eaten for dessert. The *Challah* is baked in a round shape (reminding us of eternity) instead of a braid and is enriched with extra eggs, sugar, and raisins to signify the promise for a sweet and rich year. *Gefilte Fish*, chicken soup with three-cornered *Kreplach* (said to symbolize the three patriarchs), carrot or prune *Tzimmes*, and meat or fowl would complete the meal.

On the eve of Yom Kippur, it is important to serve a filling meal without provoking thirst. The meal is similar to that of Rosh Hashanah less some of the sweets. The meal is eaten before the onset of Yom Kippur. It is called *Se-udah Mafseket*, the concluding meal before a fast. There is no *Kiddush*, and the festival candles are lit after the meal and before going to the synagogue. A light dairy dinner is often eaten after the fast, consisting of assorted fish, eggs, and salads.

The Sukkot table is laden with the fruits and vegetables of the fall harvest. Stuffed foods of all kinds are served to symbolize the richness of the harvest. Cabbage filled with ground beef in a sweet and sour sauce, *Holishkes* (or *Gefilte Kraut*), are popular among Ashkenazic Jews. Israelis stuff eggplants (*Chatsilim*) and green peppers (*Pilpel Memula*). Strudel stuffed with apples, peaches, or other fruits is served for dessert.

Chanukah is celebrated by eating foods cooked in oil, such as potato *Latkes* (potato pancakes) and *Sufganyot* (jelly doughnuts) to symbolize the miracle of the oil. It is also customary to eat dairy dishes in remembrance of the story of Judith in the Apocrypha.

Hamantaschen, a three-cornered pastry filled with prunes, poppy seeds (*Muhn*), apricots, or other fruits, is the most popular of Purim foods. It is three-cornered, tradition says, to look like Haman's ears or like the purse he wanted to fill with the Jews' gold. Haman's ears are a favorite Purim dessert. They are a fritter-like pastry, deep-fried, and sprinkled with sugar or honey. They are known as *Hamansooren* in Holland, *Orechie de Aman* in Italy, *Oznei Haman* in Israel, and *Honuelos de Haman* in Spanish-speaking countries.

The *Seder* is a celebration and learning experience shared by all present. The special foods served enhance the beauty and the meaning of the night. Passover foods vary in Sephardic and Ashkenazic communities. Ashkenazim exclude rice while Sephardim serve rice. Ashkenazim also exclude millet, corn, and legumes (beans and nuts). The Rabbis thought that the seed inside the bean would "rise" like leavening. Since no leaven (*Chamets*) may be used, *Matzah* is the main ingredient of Passover cooking. There is a rich variety of foods made from *Matzah* and *Matzah* meal. Ashkenazic favorites are *Kneidlach* (*Matzah* meal dumplings), *Matzah Brei* (fried *Matzah* with egg and onion), and *Kremslach* (*Matzah* meal fritters), which recall the meal cakes offered as sacrifices in Biblical times. *Matzah* meal or potato flour is used instead of flour.

Sephardic dishes are *Fahthut*, a Yemenite soup stew made with *Matzah* meal, and Turkish *Minas* and *Mahmuras*, layers of *Matzah* filled with vegetables, cheese, or meat.

Dairy foods are served on Shavuot. According to legend, after our ancestors received the Torah on Mt. Sinai, they returned to their tents too hungry to wait for meat to be cooked so they ate previously prepared dairy dishes. Milk, cheese, and honey are the favorite foods of this festival. The sweet dishes made from cheese and honey symbolize the sweetness and richness of the Torah. Popular dishes are *Blintzes* stuffed with cheese, cheese-filled strudel, beet *Borsht* served with sour cream, *Kugel* (noodle pudding), and cheese cake. Sephardic Jews serve dishes like *Shpongous* (a cheese-spinach bake), sometimes using salted ewe's milk.

Our festivals are always enhanced through the rich tastes and texures of the holiday foods. The beauty and delight of these specially prepared meals add a great deal to the *Hidur Mitzvah*, the aesthetic enjoyment of our holidays.

◆ ◆

HIDUR MITZVAH: THE AESTHETICS OF *MITZVOT*

THE sources delineate the minimum requirements of the *mitzvot*. A *Sukkah* must have certain dimensions and must be constructed in a particular manner. The cup for *Kiddush* must be large enough to hold a specified minimum amount of wine. While some may be satisfied with minimum standards, the Jewish tradition recognizes and encourages the addition of an aesthetic dimension. Beauty enhances the *mitzvot* by appealing to the senses. Beautiful sounds and agreeable fragrances, tastes, textures, colors, and artistry contribute to human enjoyment of religious acts, and beauty itself takes on a religious dimension. The principle of enhancing a *mitzvah* through aesthetics is called *Hidur Mitzvah*.

The concept of *Hidur Mitzvah* is derived from Rabbi Ishmael's comment on the verse, "This is my God and I will glorify Him" (Exodus 15:2).

> Is it possible for a human being to add glory to his Creator?
> What this really means is: I shall glorify Him in the way I perform
> *mitzvot*. I shall prepare before Him a beautiful *Lulav*, a beautiful
> *Sukkah*, beautiful fringes (*Tsitsit*), and beautiful phylacteries (*Te-
> filin*).[1]

The Talmud adds to this list a beautiful *Shofar* and a beautiful Torah scroll which has been written by a skilled scribe with fine ink and fine pen and wrapped in beautiful silks.[2]

"In keeping with the principle of *Hidur Mitzvah*," Rabbi Zera taught, "one should be willing to pay even one third more [than the normal price]."[3]

---

[1]Midrash *Mechilta, Shirata*, chapter III, ed. Lauterbach, page 25.
[2]Talmud B., *Shabbat* 133b.
[3]Talmud B., *Bava Kama* 9b.

Jewish folklore is replete with stories about Jews of modest circumstances paying more than they could afford for the most beautiful *Etrog* to enhance their observance of Sukkot, or for the most delectable foods to enhance their observance of Shabbat.

The Midrash suggests that not only are *mitzvot* enhanced by an aesthetic dimension but so is the Jew who observes it: "*You are beautiful, my love, you are beautiful,* through *mitzvot* . . . beautiful through *mitzvot,* beautiful through deeds of loving kindness, . . . through prayer, through reciting the "*Shema,*" through the *Mezuzah,* through phylacteries, through *Sukkah* and *Lulav* and *Etrog*. . . ."[4] There seems to be reciprocity of beauty through the agency of *mitzvot:* the Jew becomes beautiful as he/she performs a *mitzvah.* "But, conversely, Israel 'beautifies' God by performing the commandments in the most 'beautiful' manner. . . ."[5]

There are many ways to apply the principle of *Hidur Mitzvah.* For example, one might choose to observe the *mitzvah* of kindling Chanukah lights with a cheap, stamped tin *Chanukiyah* or one might make an effort to build one by hand or to buy a beautiful one. Some families might prefer an oil-burning *Chanukiyah,* rather than one that uses the standard candles, in order to relate their observance of the *mitzvah* more closely to the times of the Maccabees. Certainly the *mitzvah* of lighting Chanukah candles is fulfilled with any kind of *Chanukiyah,* but by applying the principle of *Hidur Mitzvah,* one enriches both the *mitzvah* and him/herself.

Various companies distribute free *Haggadot* to their customers before Pesach. These *Haggadot* generally contain the entire traditional text and of course may be used at the family *Seder.* But a family who is motivated by the concept of *Hidur Mitzvah* will want to use one of the beautifully edited and illustrated *Haggadot* readily available today (for example, *A Passover Haggadah,* published by the CCAR, edited by Herbert Bronstein and illustrated by Leonard Baskin). Alternatively, a family or group of families may wish to edit and illustrate their own *Haggadah.* Similarly, beautiful *Matzah* covers, *Seder* plates, and *Kiddush* cups should be used. These may be family heirlooms, or ones created by contemporary artists, or ones designed and executed by the children in religious school. The whole cele-

---

[4]Midrash *Song of Songs Rabbah* 1.15.
[5]Montefiore and Loewe, *A Rabbinic Anthology* (London: 1938), note by H. Loewe, page 118.

bration is enriched when care is taken in the selection or creation of cer emonial objects.

. Affixing a *Mezuzah* to the doorpost of a Jewish house is a *mitzvah* (see *Gates of Mitzvah*, page 38, E-4). The concept of *Hidur Mitzvah* suggests that the *Mezuzah* be artistically fashioned. If one's eye is attracted by the beauty of the *Mezuzah*, one will be more likely to consider its significance (i.e., that as one enters, he pauses to think of God). Some might even study the traditions relating to the writing of a *Mezuzah* and then lovingly create their own *Mezuzah*. *Hidur Mitzvah* means taking the time and making an effort to create or acquire the most beautiful ceremonial objects possible in order to enrich the religious observance with aesthetic dimension.

◆ ◆

ON CHOOSING JUDAISM AND CHOOSING *MITZVOT*

JOSEPH EDELHEIT

THE person who has chosen to join the Jewish people or has chosen to share his or her life with a Jew approaches the *mitzvot* with an attitude different from that of the born Jew. No matter how little Jewish education a born Jew might have, he or she knows that there is a vast body of Jewish custom and tradition. If one partakes of it, one's Judaism is deepened and enriched; if one ignores it, it is still part of the Jewish heritage that one may someday reclaim. This is, of course, not true for the person not raised as a Jew but who, as an adult, has either chosen Judaism or chosen to be part of a Jewish family. How or why should the person without "Jewish memory" choose to do certain *mitzvot*?

For anyone seeking an answer to this question, the key is to find individuals who are willing to act as guides, role models, and friends. The synagogue and its rabbi is the place to begin. The rabbi will be able to provide information about study programs, workshops, and books such as this one which will help clarify the meaning and detail of the observance of *mitzvot*. The rabbi will also suggest members of the community who will be glad to help a person learn the basic skills of Jewish living. One's own Jewish family can be a rich source of information and aid. Through the sympathetic care and concern of others—initial awkwardness, embarrassment, and discomfort can be overcome.

During the early stages of one's introduction to Judaism, *mitzvot* such as lighting candles, reciting *Kiddush*, building a *Sukkah*, or preparing a *Seder* may seem like overwhelming tasks, but by observing others and then attempting them by oneself an individual gains confidence. Whenever one attempts something new or unfamiliar, one may make mistakes. It is a part of the learning process. The repetition of the *mitzvot* will establish them as a part of the pattern of living. The secret is to begin, to repeat them, and then add more when one can.

The mechanics of the *mitzvot* are relatively easy to master, but it is natural especially at the outset not to "feel" Jewish. A new identity takes time to build, and it requires patience; as one becomes comfortable with performing a particular *mitzvah*, one should focus one's attention on its meaning. This is called doing a *mitzvah* with *Kavanah*. For example, by concentrating on the meaning of the *Seder*, one will gradually feel the movement from slavery to freedom. Jewish memories are formed from Jewish experience. For some the process will be quite rapid; for others it will be more gradual.

The performance of many *mitzvot* involves the recitation of blessings. Blessings may be recited in Hebrew or in English. Hebrew is both *Leshon Hakodesh*, The Holy Tongue, the language of our sacred literature—Torah, Talmud, *Siddur*, etc.—and the living language of our people in Israel. To learn Hebrew is a *mitzvah* (see *Gates of Mitzvah*, page 20, E-6), and knowing it enriches one's Jewish life. One may begin by reciting the blessings in English. Then, as one becomes more familiar with the *mitzvot*, one may wish to learn the blessings by the use of transliteration or by the many tapes and records which are available. Friends who know the blessings will also be pleased to help. For those who want to learn Hebrew, many synagogues, Jewish community centers, and local colleges have courses available. It is to be hoped that born Jews who rediscover *mitzvot* and those who choose Judaism will decide to learn Hebrew because of its central role in the religious and cultural life of the Jewish people.

By observing *mitzvot* one adds a new dimension to life. As one participates in the celebration of festivals and holy days, one experiences the joy, sadness, and meaning associated with each occasion. During the vast majority of the year, Jews who have recently chosen Judaism or non-Jews living in a Jewish family, may find little or no difficulty with the decision they made. However, some have found that the December holiday season can often be confusing and painful. While they observe the Chanukah *mitzvot* with great joy and enthusiasm, the warm family memories associated with Christmas, as well as societal emphasis on the social and commercial aspects of the day, fill them with a sense of loss. Lydia Kukoff, in her book *Choosing Judaism* (New York, UAHC, 1981, pages 69–72), describes her feelings of discomfort and those of others whom she interviewed. While there are no general answers which fit every set of circumstances, she recommends:

> Immerse yourself in Chanukah. Buy a Chanukiah (menorah), invite friends over for candle lighting. Make latkes. Learn to spin a dreidel. Sing. And especially come to appreciate this holiday of dedication and freedom which embodies an important lesson for our society—the possibility that few *can* make a difference in face of overwhelming odds.

The "December Dilemma" is real for many and is an issue which must be discussed and understood.

All who choose to become Jews or to live in a Jewish family should be aware that their decision affects those who care for them. There is a need to be willing to share information and to deal with their non-Jewish families who may or may not want to participate in the celebration of Jewish life-cycle events and holiday observances. Understanding and concern are important in helping the family to comprehend new circumstances. Choosing Judaism does not mean rejecting one's family, but it does mean that significant changes have occurred. Patience and love can help to heal wounds and open the doors to continued warm relationships.

The key to a life of *mitzvot* is doing. It is through the performance of *mitzvot* that "Jewish memories" are constructed. Living as a Jew means doing. Feeling and memories take time to acquire. With personal resolve and the loving help of family, friends, and community, the gates of *mitzvah* are open to all who are willing to walk through them.

GLOSSARY

Adar. The twelfth month of the Jewish calendar. In a leap year, a thirteenth month—called *Adar Sheni* ("Second Adar")—is added.

Adlayada. Purim carnival. The term comes from the Aramaic words "*ad dela yada*" ("until he could not discern") included in the Talmudic phrase, "A person should be so merry on Purim that *he could not discern* between 'cursed is Haman' and 'blessed is Mordecai.' "

Afikoman. Name of the middle of the three *matzot* on the Passover *Seder* plate. It is eaten at the conclusion of the *Seder* meal. The word *Afikoman* is of Greek origin, but its exact etymology is unclear. It has been interpreted as "after-meal entertainment" or "dessert."

Ahasuerus. King of Persia whose domain, according to the Book of Esther, ranged from India to Ethiopia.

"Al chet (shechatanu lefanecha)." "For the sin (we have committed against You)." The first words of the formula of confession of sins recited on Yom Kippur.

"Al hanisim." "For the miracles." A thanksgiving prayer added to the *Amidah* during Chanukah and Purim.

"Aleinu (leshabeach)." "It is our duty (to praise [the Lord])." A prayer which originally introduced the *Malchuyot* section of the Rosh Hashanah service in which the kingship of God is proclaimed. Later, "*Aleinu*" was adopted as a standard concluding feature of the daily and holiday worship.

Am Berit. "People of the Covenant." The Jewish people.

Amidah. "Standing." The core and main element of each of the prescribed daily services. Also known as *Tefilah* and (among Ashkenazim) as *Shemoneh Esreh* ("Eighteen") because of the eighteen benedictions which it originally comprised.

Aramaic. A Semitic language, closely related to Hebrew, that was widely used in Talmudic times.

Aravah (pl.: *Aravot*). "Willow." One of the four species gathered on Sukkot.

Arba Parashiyot. "Four portions [of the Torah]" read in addition to the weekly portion on the four Sabbaths preceding Pesach.

Arba-ah Minim. "Four Species." The four species gathered during the Sukkot festival; citron (*etrog*), palm (*lulav*), myrtle (*hadas*), and willow (*aravah*).

Aseret Yemei Teshuvah. "Ten Days of Repentance." The ten-day period from Rosh Hashanah through Yom Kippur. The period is also called *Yamim Nora-im* ("Days of Awe").

"Ashamnu." "We have trespassed." The opening word of the formula of confession of sins which is part of Yom Kippur and other penitential services.

Ashkenazi (pl.: *Ashkenazim*). "German." A Jew from Central or Eastern Europe or his/her descendants.

"Ata vechartanu." "You have chosen us." The central benediction of the *Amidah* on the Festivals which affirms God's love for Israel which is expressed through His gift of the Festivals.

Atseret. "Festive meeting." The eighth day of the Sukkot festival, coinciding in Reform Judaism and in Israel with the holiday of Simchat Torah. (Orthodox Jews observe Simchat Torah on the ninth day.) Also known as *Shemini Atseret*.

Av. The fifth month of the Jewish calendar.

"Avinu, Malkenu." "Our Father, Our King." A litany recited during the Ten Days of Repentance.

Aviv. Spring. In the Bible, also the name of the month in which Pesach occurs.

Avodah. "Service." A major part of the Yom Kippur service which recalls the Yom Kippur ritual in the Temple. In the Reform prayerbook it is part of the afternoon service.

Avot (sing.: *Av*). "Fathers." The Biblical Patriarchs (Abraham, Isaac, and Jacob). Also the name of the first benediction of the *Amidah*.

Bar/Bat Mitzvah (pl.: *Benei/Benot Mitzvah*). "Subject to *Mitzvah*." The status of the thirteen-year-old who undertakes the performance of *mitzvot* for him/herself; the ceremony at which he/she is called to the Torah for the first time.

Bedikat Chamets.   "Search for *Chamets* (leavened bread)." A symbolic search for the last remains of leaven conducted on the night before the first Passover *Seder.*

Beitsah (pl.: *Beitsim*).   "Egg." One of the items on the Passover *Seder* plate. The egg represents the festival offering; it symbolizes life itself, and the triumph of life over death.

Bikur Cholim.   [The *mitzvah* of] visiting the sick.

Bikurim.   "First fruits." An ancient custom of bringing the first seasonal fruits to the Temple in Jerusalem.

Birkat Hamazon.   "Blessing of the meal." Prayers recited after eating. Grace after meals.

Birkat Hashir.   "Blessing of the song." A prayer recited at Shabbat and festival morning services at the end of the preliminary section known as *Pesukei Dezimrah* (Poems of Praise). It is also a part of the Passover *Haggadah.* Also known as "*Nishmat,*" because it begins with the words "*Nishmat kol chai*" ("The breath of every living being [shall bless Your Name]).

Blintzes.   Thin, rolled pancakes filled with cream cheese or cottage cheese, fruit, or seasoned mashed potatoes, and often served with sour cream. Eaten on Shavuot.

Bokser.   Fruit of the carob tree. Eaten on Tu BiShevat.

Borsht.   A Russian beet soup served hot or cold, often with sour cream.

Chag (pl.: *Chagim*).   Holiday, festival.

Chag Ha-asif.   "The Ingathering Festival." Sukkot.

Chag Ha-aviv.   "The Spring Festival; The Festival of the Month Aviv." Passover.

Chag Habikurim.   "The Festival of First Fruits." Shavuot.

Chag Hakatsir.   "The Harvest Festival." Shavuot.

Chag Hamatzot.   "The Festival of Unleavened Bread." Passover.

Chagigah (pl.: *Chagigot*).   Celebration. Also festive offering brought by visitors to the Temple on the Festivals.

Challah (pl.: *Challot*).   Special holiday bread. The name is derived from the special dough offering which was set aside for the priests during the existence of the Temple. After the destruction of the Temple people continued the practice of setting aside part of the dough when they baked holiday loaves. Eventually the term *challah* was applied to the holiday loaves themselves.

Chamesh Megilot. "The Five Scrolls." Five of the Biblical books which are read on holidays and festivals. Song of Songs (*Shir Hashirim*) is read on the intermediate Shabbat of Passover; Ruth is read on Shavuot; Lamentations (*Eichah*) is read on Tish-ah Be-Av; Ecclesiastes (*Kohelet*) is read on the intermediate Shabbat of Sukkot; and Esther is read on Purim.

Chamets. "Leaven." Leavened products which are not to be eaten during Passover.

Chamisha Asar BiShevat. "The Fifteenth of Shevat." See *Tu Bishevat.*

Chanukah. "Dedication; Consecration." The Feast of Lights. Chanukah begins on the 25th day of Kislev and lasts for eight days. It commemorates the victory of Judah Maccabee and his followers over the forces of the Syrian tyrant Antiochus Epiphanes (165 B.C.E.) and the rededication of the Temple in Jerusalem.

Chanukiyah (pl.: *Chanukiyot*). Eight-branched Chanukah candelabrum. Also known as "*Menorah.*"

Charoset. One of the items on the Passover *Seder* plate. A mixture of ground nuts, fruits, spices, and wine used to sweeten the bitter herbs eaten on Passover night. Symbolic of the mortar which our ancestors used for Pharaoh's labor.

Chasidei Umot Ha-olam. "The Righteous of the Nations." Benevolent Gentiles who risked or gave their lives to save Jews during the *Sho-ah* (Holocaust).

Chatsil (pl.: *Chatsilim*). Eggplant.

Chavurah (pl.: *Chavurot*). "Fellowship; community." An informal, usually small association, sometimes (but not necessarily) formed within a congregation, whose purpose is the enhancement of Judaism through shared prayer and study and the adoption of a more explicit Jewish life-style.

Cheshvan.   The eighth month of the Jewish calendar.

Chol Hamo-ed.   The intermediate days (between the first and last days) of Pesach and Sukkot.

Cholent.   Stew. Traditionally eaten during the Shabbat noon meal. In America, it typically contains brisket, onions, lima beans, and barley or potatoes.

Citron.   One of the four species gathered on Sukkot.

Confirmation.   Originally a substitution for the Bar/Bat Mitzvah ceremony, today it is held in Reform congregations on or near Shavuot as a group ceremony of commitment to the covenant. Also called *Kabbalat Torah* in Hebrew.

Consecration.   Special ceremony for children entering religious school for the first time. Most congregations hold it on Simchat Torah.

Cup of Elijah.   See *Kos Shel Eliyahu.*

Days of Awe.   See *Yamim Nora-im.*

Dreidel.   A four-sided spinning top used in Chanukah games.

Eifah.   An ancient measure of corn.

"Ein me-arevin simchah besimchah."   "One may not mix two joyous occasions." The Talmudic prohibition of holding marriages on festival days.

"El malei rachamim."   "God, full of compassion." Prayer for the dead.

"El Melech, yoshev al kise rachamim."   "Sovereign God, enthroned in mercy." Part of the liturgy for the Days of Awe.

Elijah.   Israelite prophet active during the reign of Ahab and Ahaziah (9th century B.C.E.). According to Jewish folklore, Elijah appears on the eve of Passover to bring his message of redemption.

Elul.   The sixth month of the Jewish calendar.

Erev (pl.: *Aravim*).   "Evening, eve." The time prior to the start of Shabbat or the festival. All Jewish holidays begin at night. Thus, for example, *"Erev Shabbat"* refers to Friday, especially the afternoon and early evening before the beginning of Shabbat; *"Erev Sukkot"* is the day before the first day of Sukkot. However, in popular parlance the first night of the holiday is often referred to as *"Erev Sukkot,"* etc.

Esther.   Heroine of the Book of Esther. Also known as Hadassah. Through her actions Haman's plan to annihilate the Jewish people was thwarted.

Etrog (pl.: *Etrogim*).   "Citron." One of the four species gathered on Sukkot.

Fahthut.   A Yemenite Passover dish.

Fast of Esther.   See *Ta-anit Ester.*

Fast of Gedaliah.   A fast day on the 3rd day of Tishri. It commemorates the murder of Gedaliah ben Ahikam who was appointed governor of Judah by Nebuchadnezzar after the first destruction of Jerusalem (586 B.C.E.). Reform Jews do not observe this day.

Five Scrolls.   See *Chamesh Megilot.*

Four Cups.   Participants in the Passover *Seder* are required to drink four cups of wine. The four cups correspond to the four parts of the *Seder*: *Kiddush* and the Blessing of Redemption before the meal, and *Birkat Hamazon* and *Birkat Hashir* after the meal.

Four Questions.   Part of the Passover *Haggadah*. It is customary for the youngest participant(s) in the *Seder* to recite the Four Questions.

Four Species.   See *Arba-ah Minim.*

Gefilte Fish.   "Filled Fish." Chopped fish mixed with crumbs, eggs, and seasonings, cooked in a broth and usually served chilled in the form of balls or oval-shaped cakes. Part of the traditional Shabbat evening meal.

Gefilte Kraut.   "Filled Cabbage." Cabbage leaves filled with ground meat. Part of the traditional Sukkot meal.

"Gemar chatimah tova!"   "May you be signed and sealed in the Book of Life for a good year!" Greeting for Yom Kippur.

Gregger.   A noisemaker used to drown out the sound of Haman's name during the reading of the Scroll of Esther on Purim.

Hachnasat Orechim.   [The *mitzvah* of] hospitality to guests.

Hadar.   "Beautiful." Rabbinic interpretation identifies the fruit of the "*hadar* tree" (Leviticus 23:40) as the *etrog* (citron). It is one of the four species gathered on Sukkot.

Hadas (pl.: *Hadasim*). "Myrtle." One of the four species gathered on Sukkot.

Hadlakat Hanerot. [The *mitzvah* of] kindling of the candles [on the eve of Shabbat and festivals].

Haftarah (pl.: *Haftarot*). "Conclusion." A section from the prophetic books of the Bible read on Shabbat and holidays after the reading of the Torah.

Haggadah (pl.: *Haggadot*). "Narrative." The tale of the Exodus from Egypt read on Passover night.

Hallel. Psalms 113–118 recited on Rosh Chodesh and the Festivals.

Haman. The vizier in the court of King Ahasuerus who sought the annihilation of the Jewish people because Mordecai, Queen Esther's cousin, refused to prostrate himself before him.

Hamansooren. Dutch name for *Hamantaschen.*

Hamantaschen. Three-cornered pastry filled with prunes, poppy seeds, apricots, or other fruits. A Purim dessert symbolizing Haman's ears or pockets.

Hama-or Hagadol. "The Bigger Light." The sun.

Hama-or Hakatan. "The Lesser Light." The moon.

"Hamotsi." "He Who brings forth [bread]." The benediction recited over bread and before eating.

Havdalah. "Separation." The ceremony which marks the end of Shabbat and festivals. The *Havdalah* blessing separates the holy from the ordinary.

Hechag. "The Festival." Sukkot.

Hidur Mitzvah. The principle of enhancing a *mitzvah* through aesthetics.

Hin. An ancient measure of liquid.

Hoda-ah. "Thanksgiving." One of the benedictions in the *Amidah.*

Holishkes. Cabbage leaves filled with ground meat. Part of the traditional Sukkot meal.

Honeulos de Haman.   Spanish name for *Hamantaschen.*

Hoshana Rabbah.   The seventh day of Sukkot.

Hoshanot.   Clusters of willows carried in procession on the last day of Sukkot.

Iyar.   The second month of the Jewish calendar.

Jubilee.   In the Bible, a year of rest to be observed by the Israelites every fiftieth year.

Judah Hanasi.   "Judah the Prince" (later half of the 2nd century C.E.). Editor of the Mishnah. Also known as "Rabbi."

Kaparah (pl.: *Kaparot*).   "Forgiveness, absolution, expiation." The setting aside of charity money before sunset on the eve of Yom Kippur. Implicit in this act of *Kaparah* is the idea that the charity money serves as atonement for one's sins. The concept of *Kaparah* is probably based on the ancient scapegoat ritual for Yom Kippur (Leviticus 16:5–22). In later times the custom of *Kaparot* developed. One day before Yom Kippur, a person would swing a fowl around his/her head and recite the formula: "This is my substitute . . . This cock [or hen] shall meet death but I shall find a long and pleasant life of peace." The fowl was then slaughtered and given to the poor. This ritual is still practiced today in certain Orthodox circles. A variation of this rite was the substitution of money for the fowl.

Karaites.   Jewish sect which came into being at the beginning of the eighth century. Its doctrine is characterized primarily by its denial of the Talmudic-Rabbinic tradition.

Karpas.   "Parsley, green herbs." One of the items on the Passover *Seder* plate. It symbolizes the growth of springtime and the green of hope and renewal.

Kasha.   Buckwheat groats.

Kashrut.   "Fitness." The term is most often applied to the traditional Jewish dietary laws, but it might also refer to the fitness of religious objects.

Kavanah.   "Directed Intention." The state of mental concentration and devotion at prayer and during the performance of *mitzvot.*

Kedoshim (sing.: *Kadosh*). "Holy ones." Jewish martyrs.

Kedushah. "Holiness." The Hebrew word has also the connotation of separation, setting aside.

Kelal Yisra-el. The Jewish community as a whole. A term employed when discussing the common responsibility, destiny, and kinship of all members of the Jewish community.

Ketubah (pl.: *Ketubot*). The Jewish marriage contract.

Kiddush. "Sanctification." Prayers recited, usually over wine, to mark the holiness of Shabbat or festivals. The word is also used as a general term for the festive table after a morning service on such days.

Kiddush HaShem. "Sanctification of God's Name." The term denotes martyrdom, since the readiness to sanctify God's Name has its most dramatic expression in the willingness to die as a martyr.

Kislev. The ninth month of the Jewish calendar.

Kneidlach. Matzah meal dumplings.

"*Kol Nidrei.*" "All Vows." A declaration of annulment of all vows with which the evening service of Yom Kippur begins.

Kos Shel Eliyahu. "Cup of Elijah." A cup of wine placed on the Passover *Seder* table for the prophet Elijah, the herald of redemption, who, by tradition, is believed to visit every Jewish home on the first night of Passover.

Kremslach. Matzah meal fritters.

Kreplach. Three-cornered meat-filled dumplings served in soup.

Kugel. Noodle or potato pudding.

Lag Ba-Omer. The thirty-third day of the counting of the *Omer* (falling on the 18th day of Iyar). A semi-holiday during the mourning period between Passover and Shavuot.

Lashuv. To return; to repent.

Latkes. Potato pancakes traditionally served during Chanukah.

Leap Year. A year in which a second month of Adar is added. This occurs seven times in a 19-year period.

Lechem Mishneh. "Two Loaves." The two traditional loaves set out in the ancient Temple during Shabbat and festivals.

Lekach. Honey and spice cake.

"Leshanah tovah techatemu!" "May you be sealed in the Book of Life for a good year!" Greeting for Rosh Hashanah.

"Leshanah tovah tikatevu!" See *"Leshana Tovah techatemu."*

Leshon Hakodesh. "The Holy Tongue." The Hebrew language.

Lulav (pl.: *Lulavim*). "Palm Branch." One of the four species to be gathered on Sukkot. Also refers to the combination of the palm, myrtle, and willow which are taken up and waved together.

Ma-ariv. The evening service.

Maccabee. The additional name given to Judah, the military leader of the revolt against Syria in 168 B.C.E. The name Maccabee is also applied loosely to other members of the family, as well as to the Hasmonean dynasty as a whole.

Machzor (pl.: *Machzorim*). "Cycle." Festival prayerbook.

Mahmuras. Turkish dish. Layers of *Matzah* filled with vegetables, cheese, or meat.

Maimonides. Rabbi Moses ben Maimon (1135–1204), also known by the acronym Rambam. The foremost Jewish thinker and rabbinic authority of the Middle Ages. His writings include the *Guide of the Perplexed,* the *Mishneh Torah* (also known as the *Yad*), and *Sefer Hamitzvot.*

Malchuyot. "Kingdom Verses." The first of the three central benedictions of the *Shofar* service on Rosh Hashanah morning. (The other two benedictions are known as *Zichronot* and *Shofarot.*)

Mar-it Ayin. "Appearance of the Eye." The avoidance of acts which although they are not in fact prohibited by the Halachah, give the appearance of a violation.

Maror. "Bitter herbs." One of the items on the Passover *Seder* plate. The top part of the horseradish root, symbolic of the bitterness that our ancestors experienced in Egypt.

Matan Torah. "The Giving of the Torah." The revelation on Mount Sinai.

Matzah (pl.: *Matzot*).   Unleavened bread eaten during Passover and especially at the *Seder*.

Matzah Balls.   Balls made of *Matzah* meal and served in soup during Passover.

Matzah Brei.   Fried *Matzah* with eggs and onions.

Megilah (pl.: *Megilot*).   Scroll. See also *Chamesh Megilot*.

Menorah (pl.: *Menorot*).   "Candelabrum." The name given to the seven-branched candelabrum which was a prominent feature in the Tabernacle as well as in the Jerusalem Temple. Also one of the names for the eight-branched Chanukah lamp (*Chanukiyah*).

Menuchah.   "Rest." Shabbat is a day of rest.

Me-ot Chitin.   "Wheat money." Collection made before Passover to ensure a supply of flour for *Matzot* for the poor.

Mezuzah (pl.: *Mezuzot*).   "Doorpost." A scroll with Biblical verses, usually in a wooden or metal container, affixed to the doorpost of a Jewish home.

Minas.   Turkish dish for Passover.

Minchah.   The afternoon service.

Minhag (pl.: *Minhagim*).   "Custom, usage." An observance passed down through the generations, often assuming the power of law.

Mishloach Manot.   See *Shalach Mones*.

Mitzvah (pl.: *Mitzvot*).   "Commandment." Good deed, religious duty.

Mizbeach Me-at.   "A Miniature Altar." In Rabbinic writings, the family table is often compared to the altar of the Temple.

Mo-ed (pl.: *Mo-adim*).   Season; festival.

Mordecai.   A Jew who lived in Shushan, the residence of the Persian king Ahasuerus (Xerxes I) who reigned from 486 to 465 B.C.E. He was the foster father to his cousin Esther who was chosen by the king to replace the deposed queen, Vashti. Mordecai was the only one who refused to bow down to Haman, the king's vizier.

Muhn.   Poppy seeds.

Myrtle.   One of the four species gathered on Sukkot.

"*Na-aseh Venishma.*"   "We will faithfully do." Part of the phrase in Exodus 24:7, "And they [the People of Israel] said: 'All that the Lord has spoken, will we do and obey.' "

Ne-ilah.   "Conclusion, closing." The concluding prayer, recited close to sunset, on Yom Kippur.

Ner (pl.: *Nerot*).   Candle.

Ner(ot) Shel Chanukah.   Chanukah candle(s).

Ner(ot) Shel Shabbat.   Shabbat candle(s).

Nes Gadol Haya Po.   "A Great Miracle Happened Here." In Israel, the four Hebrew letters *Nun, Gimel, He,* and *Pe* on the *Dreidel* stand for *Nes Gadol Haya Po.*

Nes Gadol Haya Sham.   "A Great Miracle Happened There." In the Diaspora, the four Hebrew letters *Nun, Gimel, He,* and *Shin* on the *Dreidel* stand for *Nes Gadol Haya Sham.*

Neshamah Yeterah.   "An additional soul." According to Rabbinic legend, an additional soul dwells in the Jew during Shabbat.

Nisan.   The first month of the Jewish calendar.

"*Nishmat (kol chai).*"   "The soul (of every living being)." The opening words and the name of a prayer recited at Shabbat and festival morning services at the end of the preliminary section of the service called *Pesukei Dezimrah* (Poems of Praise). It is also a part of the Passover *Haggadah.* Also known as "*Birkat Hashir.*"

Omer.   "Sheaf; wave offering." The wave offering brought to the Temple on the 16th day of Nisan, and thus the name of the 49-day period between Passover and Shavuot. Traditionally, the forty-nine days of the *Omer* are considered a period of semi-mourning because, according to the Talmud, 12,000 of Rabbi Akiba's disciples were killed between Passover and Shavuot during the Hadrianic persecution which followed the Bar Kochba revolt. The majority of Reform congregations take no special note of this period.

Oneg.   "Joy, delight." Shabbat is a day of *Oneg.* The term also refers to the social gathering after a Shabbat evening service or to a study session and get-together on Shabbat afternoon.

Orechie de Aman. Italian name for *Hamantaschen.*

Oznei Haman. Hebrew name for *Hamantaschen.*

Palm. One of the four species to be gathered on Sukkot.

Pesach. "Passover." Spring festival, beginning on the 15th day of Nisan and lasting for seven days. It commemorates the Israelite Exodus from Egypt, with the concept of freedom as its main theme. It is called "Pesach" or "Passover" because God "passed over" or protected the houses of the children of Israel. *Pesach* is also the paschal lamb that was offered as a scarifice on the eve of the feast in Temple times.

Phylacteries. See *Tefilin.*

Pilgrimage Festivals. A collective name for Passover, Shavuot, and Sukkot (including Atseret/Simchat Torah).

Pilpel Memula. Stuffed green pepper.

Pirkei Avot. "Ethics of the Fathers." The tractate Avot of the Mishnah.

Pitmah (pl.: *Petamot*). "Nipple." The tip of the *etrog* (citron).

Purim. "Lots." The holiday commemorating the deliverance of the Jews of ancient Persia from Haman's plot to kill them, through the efforts of Mordecai and Queen Esther. Purim ("lots") is so called after the lots cast by Haman in order to determine the month in which the slaughter was to take place. The holiday is celebrated on the 14th day of Adar. (In leap years it is celebrated during the Second Adar.)

Ra-ashan (pl.: *Ra-ashanim*). Hebrew name for *Gregger.*

Rama. Rabbi Moses Isserles (1520–1572). Best known for his commentary on the *Shulchan Aruch* called the "*Mappah.*" He provides Ashkenazi traditions to Caro's work.

Rashi. Rabbi Solomon Yitzhaki (1040–1105), the leading medieval Bible and Talmud commentator.

Rosh Chodesh. "The New Moon, The New Month." The first day of the month.

Rosh Hashanah. The Jewish New Year. Celebrated on the first day of Tishri. The holiday initiates a period of soul-searching and reflection that culminates on Yom Kippur.

Samaritans. Members of a religious community claiming to be descendants of the Ten Tribes. Their religion, they claim, represents the true teachings of Moses, since they accept the Pentateuch alone as holy scripture. They identify the "chosen place" of God with Mount Gerizim, overlooking Shechem (Nablus).

Sechach. "Thatch." The branches and plants covering the *Sukkah.*

Seder (pl.: *Sedarim*). "Order, arrangement." The family meal and home ritual for Passover.

Sefirat Ha-omer. "Counting of the *Omer.*" Counting the forty-nine days between the second day of Passover and Shavuot.

Selichot (sing.: *Selicha*). In the singular, the word means "forgiveness." In the plural, it designates special penitential prayers which are recited during the penitential season which begins before Rosh Hashanah and concludes with Yom Kippur. A special *Selichot* service is recited late on the Saturday before Rosh Hashanah.

Sephardi (pl.: *Sephardim*). "Spaniard." A Jew who is derived from the Iberian peninsula. The term is often erroneously used to designate all Jews who are non-Ashkenazi.

Se-udah Mafseket. The last meal before the Yom Kippur fast begins.

Seventeenth of Tamuz. A fast day. According to the Mishnah, "on the seventeenth of Tamuz the Ten Commandments were smashed, the Daily Whole Offerings ceased, the City of Jerusalem was breached, and Apostomus burnt the Torah and an idol was set up in the Temple." Reform Jews do not observe this day.

Sevivon (pl.: *Sevivonim*). Hebrew name for *Dreidel.*

Shabbat (pl.: *Shabbatot*). The Sabbath; Saturday; the seventh day of the week; an occasion for rest and spiritual refreshment, abstention from the concerns of the workaday world, and participation in home and synagogue religious observances.

Shabbat Hachodesh. "Sabbath of the Month." The Shabbat immediately preceding the month of Nisan. It announces the arrival of Nisan and serves as part of the preparations for Passover.

Shabbat Hagadol. "The Great Sabbath." The Shabbat immediately preceding Passover.

Shabbat Parah. The Shabbat preceding *Shabbat Hachodesh.* It recalls the purification ritual of the Red Heifer (*Parah Adumah*).

Shabbat Shabbaton. "Sabbath of Sabbaths." The Bible refers only to Shabbat and Yom Kippur by this name.

Shabbat Shekalim. The Shabbat immediately preceding the month of Adar. During this Shabbat, Exodus 30:11–16 is read in addition to the weekly Torah portion. These verses contain the warning that the half-*Shekel* tax paid to support the Temple was due. The giving of *Tzedakah* at Purim is linked to the ancient half-*Shekel* tax.

Shabbat Shuvah. The Shabbat between Rosh Hashanah and Yom Kippur. Its name is derived from the first word of the *Haftarah* (Hosea 14:2–10), which begins "*Shuvah Yisra-el*" ("Return, O Israel").

Shabbat Zachor. "Sabbath of Remembrance." The Shabbat immediately preceding Purim. The additional Torah reading for this Shabbat (Deuteronomy 25:17–19) begins with the words "*Zachor et asher asa lecha Amalek*" ("Remember what Amalek did to you"). *Shabbat Zachor* serves as a preparation for Purim.

Shabbaton. Complete rest; total cessation of work.

Shacharit. The morning prayer.

Shalach Mones. "Sending of Portions." A Purim custom of exchanging gifts of food or pastries with friends and family. Also known as "*Mishloach Manot*."

Shalosh Regalim. The three Pilgrimage Festivals. A collective name for Passover, Shavuot, and Sukkot (including Atseret/Simchat Torah), on which pilgrims used to ascend to Jerusalem.

Shamash. "Servant." The auxiliary candle used to light the eight Chanukah candles.

Shamor. "Observe." In Deuteronomy 5:12 we are commanded, "*Shamor et yom haShabbat lekadesho*" ("Observe the Sabbath day to keep it holy").

"*Shavua Tov!*"   "Have a good week!" A greeting at the end of the *Havdalah* service at the conclusion of Shabbat.

Shavuot.   "Weeks." A festival celebrated on the 6th day of Sivan, seven weeks ("a week of weeks") after Passover. The holiday is also called *Chag Hakatsir* ("The Harvest Festival"), *Chag Habikurim* ("The Festival of First Fruits"), and *Zeman Matan Toratenu* ("The Season of the Giving of the Torah").

"*Shehecheyanu.*"   "Who has kept us alive." Key word in a special blessing of gratitude recited on holidays and occasions of joy.

"*Shema (Yisra-el).*"   "Hear (O Israel)." The central affirmation of the Jewish liturgy, taken from Deuteronomy 6:4–9.

"*Shema Kolenu.*"   "Hear Our Voice." Part of the liturgy for the Days of Awe.

Shemini Atseret.   "The eighth day of the festive meeting." See *Atseret.*

Shemoneh Esreh.   "Eighteen." See *Amidah.*

Shevarim.   "Broken sounds." One of the sounds produced by the *Shofar*— an alternation of higher and lower notes.

Shevat.   The eleventh month of the Jewish calendar.

Shiv-ah.   "Seven." The seven days of mourning for family members.

Shofar (pl.: *Shofarot*).   An animal's horn prepared for use as the ritual horn on Rosh Hashanah and Yom Kippur.

Shofarot.   "*Shofar* Verses." The last of the three central benedictions of the *Shofar* service on Rosh Hashanah morning. (The other two benedictions are known as *Malchuyot* and *Zichronot.*)

Shpongous.   A cheese-spinach bake served by Sephardim on Shavuot.

Shushan Purim.   The 15th day of Adar. So called because, according to the Book of Esther, the Jews of Shushan celebrated Purim on the 15th rather than on the 14th day of Adar.

Siddur (pl.: *Siddurim*).   "Arrangement." Prayerbook.

Sidrah (pl.: *Sedarot*). "Order; arrangement." Popular term for the sections of the Pentateuch read publicly in the synagogue on Shabbat.

"*Sim Shalom*." "Give Peace." A prayer for peace at the end of the *Amidah*.

Simchah (pl.: *Semachot*). Joy, rejoicing, happiness; festivity, joyful occasion.

Simchat Torah. "Rejoicing of the Torah." The festival marking the annual completion and recommencing of the Torah-reading cycle. In Reform Judaism and in Israel it coincides with (Shemini) Atseret.

Sivan. The third month of the Jewish calendar.

Siyum HaTorah. "Completion of the Torah." Completion of the Torah-reading cycle on Atseret/Simchat Torah.

Song of the Sea. Exodus 14:30–15:21. Read on Passover.

Strudel. A kind of pastry made with fruit or cheese rolled up in a very thin sheet of dough and baked.

Sufganiya (pl.: *Sufganiyot*). "Doughnut." Jelly doughnut served on Chanukah.

Sukkah (pl.: *Sukkot*). "Booth." Booth erected for the festival of Sukkot in accordance with the Biblical commandment, "Ye shall dwell in booths seven days" (Leviticus 23:42).

Sukkot. "Booths, tabernacles." The autumn harvest festival which begins on the 15th day of Tishri and concludes on the 22nd with Atseret/Simchat Torah. It commemorates the *sukkot* in which the children of Israel dwelt in the wilderness after the Exodus from Egypt.

Ta-anit Ester. "The Fast of Esther." A fast day on the 13th day of Adar (the day before Purim). It probably commemorates the fast which Esther asked Mordecai to proclaim after he informed her of Haman's plot to destroy the Jews. Reform Jews do not observe this day.

Talit (pl.: *Taliyot* or *Talitot*). "Prayer Shawl." The *Talit* is usually white and made either of wool, cotton, or silk. At the four corners of the *Talit*, tassels are attached in fulfillment of the Biblical commandment of *Tsitsit*.

Talmud Torah. "The Study of Torah." The *mitzvah* of Jewish study. The term is also applied to the school where one studies Torah and Judaica.

Tamuz.   The fourth month in the Jewish calendar.

Tashlich.   "Thou shalt cast." Custom of going to a body of water on the afternoon of Rosh Hashanah and symbolically casting out one's sins. This custom is not practiced by the majority of Reform Jews.

Tayglach.   Honey and nut pastry.

Tefilah (pl.: *Tefilot*).   Prayer. Also, another name for the *Amidah.*

Tefilin.   "Phylacteries." Two black leather boxes containing Scriptural passages which are bound by black leather strips on the left arm and on the head and worn for the morning services on all days except Shabbat and Scriptural holidays.

Teki-ah.   "Blowing." One of the sounds of the *Shofar*—a glissando which begins on a lower note and swells into a higher note.

Ten Days of Repentance.   See *Aseret Yemei Teshuvah.*

Tenth of Tevet.   A fast day commemorating the beginning of the siege of Jerusalem by the Babylonian king Nebuchadnezzar. Reform Jews do not observe this day.

Teru-ah.   "Alarm." One of the sounds of the *Shofar*—a series of staccato blasts upon the lower note.

Teshuvah.   "Return." Repentance, denoting a return to God after sin.

Tevet.   The tenth month of the Jewish calendar.

Tikun Leil Shavuot.   Torah study late into the Shavuot night.

Tikun Olam.   "Putting the world aright." Reforming the universe.

Tish-ah Be-Av.   "Ninth of Av." A day of mourning commemorating the destruction of the first and second Temples in Jerusalem as well as other tragic events in Jewish history.

Tishri.   The seventh month of the Jewish calendar.

Tosafot.   "Additions." A collection of comments on the Talmud, composed in 12th–13th-century France and printed in most editions of the Talmud opposite the Rashi commentary.

Tosefta.   "Addition." A collection of Rabbinic material contemporaneous with the Mishnah but not included in it.

Tsitsit (pl.: *Tsitsiyot*).   Tassles attached to the four corners of the *Talit*.

Tu BiShevat.   "The fifteenth of Shevat." A minor holiday. This day was designated in the Mishnah as the "New Year of Trees." Also known as "Chamisha Asar BiShevat."

Tzedakah.   "Righteous act; charity." A gift given as an act of justice and moral behavior.

Tzedek.   Righteousness, justice.

Tzimmes.   A side dish of cooked vegetables or fruits.

"Unetaneh Tokef."   "Let us declare the mighty importance [of the holiness of the day]." A part of the morning service on Rosh Hashanah and Yom Kippur.

Ushpizin.   "Guests." According to Kabbalistic tradition, the seven mystical "guests" (Abraham, Isaac, Jacob, Moses, Aaron, Joseph, and David) who visit the *Sukkah* during Sukkot. Reform Judaism includes also Rebekah, Rachel, Leah, Miriam, Hannah, and Deborah.

"Ve-initem et nafshoteichem."   "Ye shall afflict your souls [on Yom Kippur]" (Leviticus 23:27). It is from this verse that the *mitzvah* of fasting on Yom Kippur is derived.

"Veshameru."   Part of the *Kiddush* for the Shabbat noon meal which begins with the words, *"Veshameru venei Yisra-el et haShabbat"* ("The Israelite people shall keep the Sabbath") (Exodus 31:16–17). It is also part of the middle blessing of the *Amidah* on Shabbat.

Vidui.   "Confession." Confessional prayers which form a central part of the Yom Kippur and *Selichot* liturgy.

Willow.   One of the four species gathered on Sukkot.

"Ya-aleh Veyavo."   "May [our remembrance] arise and come [before Thee]." The name of the additional prayer recited in the *Amidah* of Rosh Chodesh and festivals, except Rosh Hashanah and Yom Kippur.

Yamim Nora-im.   "Days of Awe." The period from the first day of Rosh Hashanah until Yom Kippur, and these two days in particular. The period is also called *Aseret Yemei Teshuvah* ("Ten Days of Repentance").

Yiddish.   Language of medieval origin developed by Ashkenazi Jews and derived from German and Eastern European dialects.

Yizkor. "He [God] shall remember." Service of remembrance for the martyrs of our people as well as for our own relatives and friends recited on Yom Kippur and the last days of the Three Pilgrimage Festivals.

Yom (pl.: *Yamim*).   Day.

Yom Ha-Atsma-ut. "Independence Day." Israel's Independence Day, celebrated on the 5th of Iyar.

Yom Hadin. "Day of Judgement." Rosh Hashanah.

Yom HaSho-ah. Holocaust Day. The 27th day of Nisan, set aside as a memorial to the victims of the Holocaust.

Yom Hazikaron. "Remembrance Day." Rosh Hashanah. In Israel, *Yom Hazikaron* refers also to a memorial day for those who fell during active duty in the Israeli War of Independence, which is observed on the 4th of Iyar (the day before *Yom Ha-Atsma-ut*).

Yom Kippur. "Day of Atonement." A solemn day of fasting and prayer concluding the ten days of penitence that begin on Rosh Hashanah. The most important day in the Jewish liturgical year.

Yom Kippur Hakatan. "The Small Yom Kippur." The seventh day of Sukkot (also known as *Hoshana Rabbah*). Tradition sees this day as an opportunity for those who have not yet completed their repentance to do so.

Yom Shekulo Shabbat. A day of eternal Shabbat. One of the traditional descriptions of the Messianic era.

Yom Yerushalayim. Jerusalem Day. Celebrated on the 28th day of Iyar. On that day, in the Six-Day War, the Israeli Defense Forces captured East Jerusalem and the city became united again.

"Zachor et asher asa lecha Amalek." "Remember what Amalek did to you." Words included in the additional Torah reading for *Shabbat Zachor* (Deuteronomy 25:17–19). In Jewish tradition Amalek is identified with Haman, the villain of the Purim story.

Zachor. "Remember." In Exodus 20:8 we are commanded, *"Zachor et yom haShabbat lekadesho"* ("Remember the Sabbath day to keep it holy").

"Zecher liytsi-at Mitsrayim." "Memorial to the Exodus from Egypt." One of the themes of the *Kiddush* for Shabbat.

Zeman cherutenu. "The season of our liberation." Passover.

Zeman matan Toratenu. "The time of the giving of the Torah." Shavuot.

Zeman simchatenu. "The season of our rejoicing." Sukkot.

Zemirot. "Songs." Special musical selections sung at the table on Shabbat and festivals.

Zeroa. A roasted shankbone burned or scorched representing the ancient Passover sacrifice. One of the items on the *Seder* plate.

Zichronot. "Remembrance Verses." The second of the three central benedictions of the *Shofar* service on Rosh Hashanah morning. (The other two benedictions are known as *Malchuyot* and *Shofarot.*)

"Zikaron lema-aseh vereshit." "Memorial to the creation of the world." One of the themes of the *Kiddush* for Shabbat.

"Zochrenu lechayim." "Remember us unto life." A Rosh Hashanah prayer.

Zuz (pl.: *Zuzim*). Silver coin; ¼ of a *Shekel.*

THE CLASSIC TEXTS
OF JUDAISM

APOCRYPHA and PSEUDEPIGRAPHA. Known in Hebrew as "hidden" works, both terms refer to collections of inter-testamental literature, c. 200 B.C.E. to 200 C.E., primarily of Jewish authorship. They are "hidden" by exclusion from the Hebrew canon. Books of the Apocrypha and Pseudepigrapha are included in some Christian Bibles.

ARBA-AH TURIM. A comprehensive compilation of private and public law, by Jacob ben Asher (1270?–1340), chiefly following the legal opinions of Maimonides and universally accepted as authoritative. The code served as the basis for Caro's monumental *Beit Yosef* and later his *Shulchan Aruch*.

GEMARA ("Completion"). A word popularly applied to the Talmud as a whole, or more particularly to the discussions and elaborations by rabbinic authorities of the 3rd to 5th centuries C.E. on the Mishnah. There is a *Gemara* to both the Bablylonian and Jerusalem Talmudim, although not to all or to the same tractates.

MIDRASH. The method of interpreting scripture to elucidate legal points (*Midrash Halachah*) or bring out lessons through stories or homiletics (*Midrash Aggadah*). "Midrash" is also the designation of a particular genre of rabbinic literature extending from pre-Mishnaic times to the 10th century. Taken together, the body of works known as "Midrash" constitutes an anthology of homilies consisting of both biblical exegesis and sermonic material. Among the more important Midrashic works are *Midrash Rabbah*[1] (separate works on each volume of the Pentateuch, c. 400–1000); *Tanchuma* (a group of homiletical Midrashim edited later than c. 800); and the *Pesikta deRav Kahana*[2] (a homiletic Midrash, probably c. 500, on portions of Scriptural readings for festivals and special Sabbaths). Among the *Midreshei Halachah*, dealing primarily

---

[1] H. Freedman and M. Simon, eds. *The Midrash*. London: Soncino Press, 1951. 10 vols.

[2] W. Braude and I. Kapstein, trans. *Pesikta deRab Kahana*. Philadelphia: Jewish Publication Society, 1975.

190 GATES OF THE SEASONS

with law as derived from the Bible, are the *Mechilta* on Exodus[3]; *Sifra* on Leviticus; and *Sifrei* on Numbers and Deuteronomy. All were edited c. 4th–5th century C.E.

MISHNAH. The first legal codification of basic Jewish law, arranged and redacted by R. Judah Hanasi about 200 C.E. The Mishnah[4] is the nucleus for all *Halachah*, and contains the basic Oral Law as evolved through generations. The Mishnah is divided into six orders: *Zera-im* (seeds), *Mo-ed* (seasons), *Nashim* (matrimonial law), *Nezikin* (civil law), *Kodashim* (holy things), and *Tohorot* (ritual purity), each order being divided into separate tractates.

MISHNEH TORAH. An encyclopedic legal code in fourteen volumes, also called *Yad Hachazakah*, by Moses ben Maimon (Maimonides; Rambam), 1135–1204. The *Mishneh Torah*[5] covers all halachic subjects discussed in the Talmud and gives clear rulings where there are conflicting opinions.

RESPONSA (Heb. *She-elot uteshuvot*). Replies sent by halachic authorities to questioners who addressed them in writing. These cover every aspect of Jewish belief and practice and are the main source for the development of Jewish law since the close of the Talmud and a primary source for Jewish and general history. The writing of responsa continues to our own day in all branches of the Jewish community.

SHULCHAN ARUCH ("A Prepared Table"). The basis for Jewish law today, by Joseph Caro (1488–1575), codifying Sephardic custom and to which was added Moses Isserles' *Mappah* ("Tablecloth"), codifying Ashkenazic custom. Usually referred to as the *Code of Jewish Law,* the *Shulchan Aruch* contains four main sub-divisions: *Orach Chayim, Yoreh De-ah, Even Ha-Ezer,* and *Choshen Mishpat.*

TALMUD ("Study" or "learning"). The body of teaching which comprises the commentary and discussions of the early Rabbis on the Mishnah of R. Judah Hanasi. Divided into the same orders and tractates as the

[3] J. Lauterbach, trs. *Mekilta*. Philadelphia: Jewish Publication Society, 1961. 3 vols.
[4] H. Danby. *The Mishnah*. London: Oxford University Press, 1933.
[5] Julian Oberman, ed. *The Code of Maimonides*. New Haven: Yale University Press, 1957, in progress.

Mishnah, the Talmudic discussions are always printed together with their corresponding parts of Mishnah. The *Babylonian Talmud*[6] is the interpretation and elaboration of Mishnah as developed in the great academies of Babylonia between the 3rd and 5th centuries, C.E., and is considered more authoritative than the smaller *Jerusalem Talmud,*[7] developed in the great academies of Palestine before the 5th century. The *Babylonian Talmud* especially, as a storehouse of Jewish history and customs as well as law, has exerted an unparalleled influence on Jewish thought and is the foundation of Judaism as we know it today.

TANACH. The traditional Hebrew acronym designating the Hebrew Bible, composed of the initial letters of the words *Torah*[8] (Pentateuch), *Neviim* (Prophets),[9] and *Ketuvim* (Writings, Hagiographa).[10]

TORAH ("Teaching, doctrine, or instruction"). The scroll consisting of the first five books of the Hebrew Bible for reading in the synagogue. "Torah" is also used to describe the entire body of traditional Jewish teaching and literature.

[6] I. Epstein, ed. *The Babylonian Talmud.* London: Soncino Press. 36 vols.
[7] J. Neusner, ed. *The Talmud of the Land of Israel.* Chicago: University of Chicago Press, 1980, in progress.
[8] G. W. Plaut. *The Torah: A Modern Commentary.* New York: UAHC, 1981.
[9] *The Prophets.* Philadelphia: Jewish Publication Society, 1978.
[10] *The Writings.* Philadelphia: Jewish Publication Society, 1982.

CALENDAR OF HOLIDAYS: 1983–1988

	5744	5745	5746	5747	5748
ROSH HASHANAH	Thurs., Sept. 8, 1983	Thurs., Sept. 27, 1984	Mon., Sept. 15, 1985	Sat., Oct. 4, 1986	Thurs., Sept. 24, 1987
YOM KIPPUR	Sat., Sept. 17, 1983	Sat., Oct. 6, 1984	Wed., Sept. 25, 1985	Mon., Oct. 13, 1986	Sat., Oct. 3, 1987
SUKKOT	Thurs., Sept. 22, to Wed., Sept. 28, 1983	Thurs., Oct. 11, to Wed., Oct. 17, 1984	Mon., Sept. 30, to Sun., Oct. 6, 1985	Sat., Oct. 18, to Fri., Oct. 24, 1986	Thurs., Oct. 8, to Wed., Oct. 14, 1987
ATSERET/SIMCHAT TORAH	Thurs., Sept. 29, 1983	Thurs., Oct. 18, 1984	Mon., Oct. 7, 1985	Sat., Oct. 25, 1986	Thurs., Oct. 15, 1987
CHANUKAH	Thurs., Dec. 1, to Thurs., Dec. 8, 1983	Wed., Dec. 19, to Wed., Dec. 26, 1984	Sun., Dec. 8, to Sun., Dec. 15, 1985	Sat., Dec. 27, 1986, to Sat., Jan. 3, 1987	Wed., Dec. 16, to Wed., Dec. 23, 1987
PURIM	Sun., March 18, 1984	Thurs., March 7, 1985	Tues., March 25, 1986	Sun., March 15, 1987	Thurs., March 3, 1988
PESACH	Tues., April 17, to Mon., April 23, 1984	Sat., April 6, to Fri., April 12, 1985	Thurs., April 24, to Wed., April 30, 1986	Tues., April 14, to Mon., April 20, 1987	Sat., April 2, to Fri., April 8, 1988
YOM HASHO-AH	Sun., April 29, 1984	Thurs., April 18, 1985	Tues., May 6, 1986	Sun., April 26, 1987	Thurs., April 14, 1988
YOM HA-ATSMA-UT	Mon., May 7, 1984	Fri., April 26, 1985	Wed., May 14, 1986	Mon., May 4, 1987	Fri., April 22, 1988
SHAVUOT	Wed., June 6, 1984	Sun., May 26, 1985	Fri., June 13, 1986	Wed., June 3, 1987	Sun., May 22, 1988
TISH-AH BE-AV	Tues., Aug. 7, 1984	Sun., July 28, 1985	Thurs., Aug. 14, 1986	Tues., Aug. 3, 1987	Sun., July 24, 1988

CALENDAR OF HOLIDAYS: 1988–1993

	5749	5750	5751	5752	5753
ROSH HASHANAH	Mon., Sept. 12, 1988	Sat., Sept. 30, 1989	Thurs., Sept. 20, 1990	Mon., Sept. 9, 1991	Mon., Sept. 28, 1992
YOM KIPPUR	Wed., Sept. 21, 1988	Mon., Oct. 9, 1989	Sat., Sept. 29, 1990	Wed., Sept. 18, 1991	Wed., Oct. 7, 1992
SUKKOT	Mon., Sept. 26, to Sun., Oct. 2, 1988	Sat., Oct. 14, to Fri., Oct. 20, 1989	Thurs., Oct. 4, to Wed., Oct. 10, 1990	Mon., Sept. 23, to Sun., Sept. 29, 1991	Mon., Oct. 12, to Sun., Oct. 18, 1992
ATSERET/SIMCHAT TORAH	Mon., Oct. 3, 1988	Sat., Oct. 21, 1989	Thurs., Oct. 11, 1990	Mon., Sept. 30, 1991	Mon., Oct. 19, 1992
CHANUKAH	Sun., Dec. 4, to Sun., Dec. 11, 1988	Sat., Dec. 23, to Sat., Dec. 30, 1989	Wed., Dec. 12, to Wed., Dec. 19, 1990	Mon., Dec. 2, to Mon., Dec. 9, 1991	Sun., Dec. 20, to Sun., Dec. 27, 1992
PURIM	Tues., March 20, 1989	Sun., March 11, 1990	Thurs., Feb. 28, 1991	Thurs., March 19, 1992	Sun., March 7, 1993
PESACH	Thurs., April 20, to Wed., April 26, 1989	Tues., April 10, to Mon., April 16, 1990	Sat., March 30, to Fri., April 5, 1991	Sat., April 18, to Fri., April 24, 1992	Tues., April 6, to Mon., April 12, 1993
YOM HASHO-AH	Tues., May 2, 1989	Sun., April 22, 1990	Thurs., April 11, 1991	Wed., April 29, 1992	Sun., April 18, 1993
YOM HA-ATSMA-UT	Wed., May 10, 1989	Mon., April 30, 1990	Fri., April 19, 1991	Fri., May 8, 1992	Mon., April 26, 1993
SHAVUOT	Fri., June 9, 1989	Wed., May 30, 1990	Sun., May 19, 1991	Sun., June 7, 1992	Wed., May 26, 1993
TISH-AH BE-AV	Thurs., Aug. 10, 1989	Tues., July 31, 1990	Sun., July 21, 1991	Sun., Aug. 9, 1992	Tues., July 27, 1993

CALENDAR OF HOLIDAYS: 1993–1998

	5754	5755	5756	5757	5758
ROSH HASHANAH	Thurs., Sept. 16, 1993	Tues., Sept. 6, 1994	Mon., Sept. 25, 1995	Sat., Sept. 14, 1996	Thurs., Oct. 2, 1997
YOM KIPPUR	Sat., Sept. 25, 1993	Thurs., Sept. 15, 1994	Wed., Oct. 4, 1995	Mon., Sept. 23, 1996	Sat., Oct. 11, 1997
SUKKOT	Thurs., Sept. 30, to Wed., Oct. 6, 1993	Tues., Sept. 20, to Mon., Sept. 26, 1994	Mon., Oct. 9, to Sun., Oct. 15, 1995	Sat., Sept. 28, to Fri., Oct. 4, 1996	Thurs., Oct. 16, to Wed., Oct. 22, 1997
ATSERET/SIMCHAT TORAH	Thurs., Oct. 7, 1993	Tues., Sept. 27, 1994	Mon., Oct. 16, 1995	Sat., Oct. 5, 1996	Thurs., Oct. 23, 1997
CHANUKAH	Thurs., Dec. 9, to Thurs., Dec. 16, 1993	Mon., Nov. 28, to Mon., Dec. 5, 1994	Mon., Dec. 18, to Mon., Dec. 25, 1995	Fri., Dec. 6, to Fri., Dec. 13, 1996	Wed., Dec. 24, to Wed., Dec. 31, 1997
PURIM	Fri., Feb. 25, 1994	Thurs., March 16, 1995	Tues., March 5, 1996	Sun., March 23, 1997	Thurs., March 12, 1998
PESACH	Sun., April 27, to Sat., May 3, 1994	Sat., April 15, to Fri., April 21, 1995	Thurs., April 4, to Wed., April 10, 1996	Tues., April 22, to Mon., April 28, 1997	Sat., April 11, to Fri., April 17, 1998
YOM HASHO-AH	Fri., April 8, 1994	Thurs., April 27, 1995	Tues., April 16, 1996	Sun., May 4, 1997	Thurs., April 23, 1998
YOM HA-ATSMA-UT	Sat., April 16, 1994	Fri., May 5, 1995	Wed., April 24, 1996	Mon., May 12, 1997	Fri., May 1, 1998
SHAVUOT	Mon., May 15, 1994	Sun., June 4, 1995	Fri., May 24, 1996	Wed., June 11, 1997	Sun., May 31, 1998
TISH-AH BE-AV	Sun., July 15, 1994	Sun., Aug. 6, 1995	Thurs., July 25, 1996	Tues., Aug. 12, 1997	Sun., Aug. 2, 1998

CALENDAR OF HOLIDAYS: 1998–2003

	5759	5760	5761	5762	5763
ROSH HASHANAH	Mon., Sept. 21, 1998	Sat., Sept. 11, 1999	Sat., Sept. 30, 2000	Tues., Sept. 18, 2001	Sat., Sept. 7, 2002
YOM KIPPUR	Wed., Sept. 30, 1998	Mon., Sept. 20, 1999	Mon., Oct. 9, 2000	Thurs., Sept. 27, 2001	Mon., Sept. 16, 2002
SUKKOT	Mon., Oct. 5, to Sun., Oct. 11, 1998	Sat., Sept. 25, to Fri., Oct. 1, 1999	Sat., Oct. 14, to Fri., Oct. 20, 2000	Tues., Oct. 2, to Mon., Oct. 8, 2001	Sat., Sept. 21, to Fri., Sept. 27, 2002
ATSERET/SIMCHAT TORAH	Mon., Oct. 12, 1998	Sat., Oct. 2, 1999	Sat., Oct. 21, 2000	Tues., Oct. 9, 2001	Sat., Sept. 28, 2002
CHANUKAH	Mon., Dec. 14, to Mon., Dec. 21, 1998	Sat., Dec. 4, to Sat., Dec. 11, 1999	Fri., Dec. 22, to Fri., Dec. 29, 2000	Mon., Dec. 10, to Mon., Dec. 17, 2001	Sat., Nov. 30, to Sat., Dec. 7, 2002
PURIM	Tues., March 2, 1999	Tues., March 21, 2000	Fri., March 9, 2001	Tues., Feb. 26, 2002	Tues., March 18, 2003
PESACH	Thurs., April 1, to Wed., April 7, 1999	Thurs., April 20, to Wed., April 26, 2000	Sun., April 8, to Sat., April 14, 2001	Thurs., March 28, to Wed., April 3, 2002	Thurs., April 17, to Wed., April 23, 2003
YOM HASHO-AH	Tues., April 13, 1999	Tues., May 2, 2000	Fri., April 20, 2001	Tues., April 9, 2002	Tues., April 29, 2003
YOM HA-ATSMA-UT	Wed., April 21, 1999	Wed., May 10, 2000	Thurs., April 26, 2001	Wed., April 17, 2002	Wed., May 7, 2003
SHAVUOT	Fri., May 21, 1999	Fri., June 9, 2000	Mon., May 28, 2001	Fri., May 17, 2002	Fri., June 6, 2003
TISH-AH BE-AV	Thurs., July 22, 1999	Thurs., Aug. 10, 2000	Sun., July 29, 2001	Thurs., July 18, 2002	Thurs., Aug. 7, 2003

CALENDAR OF HOLIDAYS: 2003–2008

	5764	5765	5766	5767	5768
ROSH HASHANAH	Sat., Sept. 27, 2003	Thurs., Sept. 16, 2004	Tues., Oct. 4, 2005	Sat., Sept. 23, 2006	Thurs., Sept. 13, 2007
YOM KIPPUR	Mon., Oct. 6, 2003	Sat., Sept. 25, 2004	Thurs., Oct. 13, 2005	Mon., Oct. 2, 2006	Sat., Sept. 22, 2007
SUKKOT	Sat., Oct. 11, to Fri., Oct. 17, 2003	Thurs., Sept. 30, to Wed., Oct. 6, 2004	Tues., Oct. 18, to Mon., Oct. 24, 2005	Sat., Oct. 7, to Fri., Oct. 13, 2006	Thurs., Sept. 27, to Wed., Oct. 3, 2007
TSERET/SIMCHAT TORAH	Sat., Oct. 18, 2003	Thurs., Oct. 7, 2004	Tues., Oct. 25, 2005	Sat., Oct. 14, 2006	Thurs., Oct. 4, 2007
CHANUKAH	Sat., Dec. 20, to Sat., Dec. 28, 2003	Wed., Dec. 8, to Wed., Dec. 15, 2004	Mon., Dec. 26, 2005, to Mon., Jan. 2, 2006	Sat., Dec. 16, to Sat., Dec. 23, 2006	Wed., Dec. 5, to Wed., Dec. 12, 2007
PURIM	Sun., March 7, 2004	Fri., March 25, 2005	Tues., March 14, 2006	Sun., March 4, 2007	Fri., March 21, 2008
PESACH	Tues., April 6, to Mon., April 12, 2004	Sun., April 24, to Sat., April 30, 2005	Thurs., April 13, to Wed., April 19, 2006	Tues., April 3, to Mon., April 9, 2007	Sun., April 20, to Sat., April 26, 2008
YOM HASHO-AH	Sun., April 18, 2004	Sat., May 6, 2005	Tues., April 25, 2006	Sun., April 15, 2007	Fri., May 2, 2008
YOM HA-ATSMA-UT	Mon., April 26, 2004	Thurs., May 12, 2005	Wed., May 3, 2006	Mon., April 23, 2007	Thurs., May 8, 2008
SHAVUOT	Wed., May 26, 2004	Mon., June 13, 2005	Fri., June 2, 2006	Wed., May 23, 2007	Mon., June 9, 2008
TISH-AH BE-AV	Tues., July 27, 2004	Sun., Aug. 14, 2005	Wed., Aug. 3, 2006	Tues., July 24, 2007	Sun., Aug. 10, 2008

FOR FURTHER READING

Agnon, S. Y.
Days of Awe. Schocken Books, 1965.

Bial, Morrison D.
Liberal Judaism at Home. UAHC, 1971.

Bickerman, E. J.
Chronology of the Ancient World. London, 1968.

Central Conference of American Rabbis.
A Shabbat Manual. CCAR, 1972.
A Passover Haggadah. CCAR, 1974.
Gates of Prayer: The New Union Prayerbook, I. CCAR, 1975.
Gates of the House: The Union Home Prayerbook. CCAR, 1977.
Gates of Understanding. CCAR, 1977.
Gates of Repentance: The New Union Prayerbook, II. CCAR, 1978.

Gaster, Theodore H.
Festivals of the Jewish Year. Morrow, 1953.

Goodman, Philip.
The Purim Anthology. Jewish Publication Society, 1949.
The Passover Anthology. Jewish Publication Society, 1961.
The Rosh Ha-Shanah Anthology. Jewish Publication Society, 1970.
The Yom Kippur Anthology. Jewish Publication Society, 1971.
The Sukkot and Simchat Torah Anthology. Jewish Publication Society, 1973.

Heschel, Abraham Joshua.
The Sabbath: Its Meaning for Modern Man. Noonday, 1975.

Millgram, Abraham E.
Sabbath: The Day of Delight. Jewish Publication Society, 1965.

Schauss, Hayyim.
The Jewish Festivals. Schocken Books, 1962.

Siegel, Richard, Michael Strassfeld, and Sharon Strassfeld.
The First Jewish Catalog. Jewish Publication Society, 1973.

Solis-Cohen, Emily.
   The Hanukah Anthology. Jewish Publication Society, 1937.
Speier, Arthur.
   The Comprehensive Hebrew Calendar. Behrman House, 1952.
Waskow, Arthur.
   Seasons of Our Joy: A Celebration of Modern Jewish Renewal. Bantam
   Books, 1982.

INDEX